D0626996

HOW THE RELIGIOUS RIGHT
SHAPED LESBIAN AND GAY ACTIVISM

Social Movements, Protest, and Contention

Series Editor   Bert Klandermans, Free University, Amsterdam

Associate Editors Ron R. Aminzade, University of Minnesota
David S. Meyer, University of California, Irvine
Verta A. Taylor, University of California, Santa Barbara

For more books in the series see page 158.

HOW THE RELIGIOUS RIGHT SHAPED LESBIAN AND GAY ACTIVISM

Tina Fetner

Social Movements, Protest, and Contention
Volume 31

University of Minnesota Press
Minneapolis • London

The University of Minnesota Press gratefully acknowledges the financial assistance provided for the publication of this book from the Dean of Social Sciences at McMaster University.

Portions of chapter 2 were previously published as "Working Anita Bryant: The Impact of Christian Antigay Activism on Lesbian and Gay Movement Claims," *Social Problems* 48, no. 3 (2001): 411–28; copyright 2001 by the Society for the Study of Social Problems; reprinted with permission of the University of California Press.

Published by the University of Minnesota Press
111 Third Avenue South, Suite 290
Minneapolis, MN 55401-2520
http://www.upress.umn.edu

Library of Congress Cataloging-in-Publication Data

Fetner, Tina.
How the religious right shaped lesbian and gay activism / Tina Fetner.
    p. cm. — (Social movements, protest, and contention ; v. 31)
Includes bibliographical references and index.
ISBN 978-0-8166-4917-4 (hc : alk. paper) — ISBN 978-0-8166-4918-1 (pb : alk. paper)
    1. Gay liberation movement—United States. 2. Gay rights—United States.
3. Religious right—United States. 4. Homophobia—United States. I. Title.
HQ76.8.U5F48 2008
306.76′6097309045—dc22
                                                           2008009096

Printed in the United States of America on acid-free paper

The University of Minnesota is an equal-opportunity educator and employer.

15 14 13 12 11 10 09 08   10 9 8 7 6 5 4 3 2 1

Contents

Acknowledgments

I owe a debt of gratitude to many people who helped me write this book. Their advice, friendship, support, and critical feedback have been invaluable. I must first thank Edwin Amenta, my incredibly supportive mentor, for many years of guidance and for nurturing this project from its earliest days. I also thank Jeff Goodwin and David F. Greenberg for their support and for reading and improving many early drafts. This book would not have been possible without their patience and hard work, and they have continued to provide encouragement and support well after their official mentoring duties were complete.

Several portions of this book were presented in some form at the New York University Sociology Department's Power, Politics, and Protest Workshop. I am grateful to Edwin Amenta, Jeff Goodwin, and James Jasper for starting this workshop, as well as to the many who participated. I must also thank colleagues from two writing groups who read and commented on several parts of this book. At NYU, the Eastern Conference All-Stars (Ellen Benoit, Chris Bonastia, and Drew Halfmann) challenged me to clarify and reconsider my theoretical perspective. At Cornell College, Cindy Benton, Michelle Mouton, and Katy Stavreva helped me develop a writing style and voice.

A number of other people read the manuscript, either partially or in full, and provided important insights in this project's development. These include Neal Caren, Kathleen Hull, Kelly Moore, Jackie Smith, Miriam Smith, and Suzanne Staggenborg. I owe special thanks to David S. Meyer, whose guidance improved the quality of this book greatly. Many others provided support through their advice, encouragement, and friendship, including Courtney

Abrams, Kim Adams, Bob Andersen, Tamara Anderson, Scott Appelrouth, Michael Armato, Christina Baade, Chip Berlet, Mary Bernstein, Jordana Engler, Jessica Fields, Dorith Geva, Brian Gifford, Adam Isaiah Green, Perry Grossman, Naomi Gunther, Amie Hess, Alana Hudson, Meika Loe, Claudia Manley, Miranda Martinez, Charlene Miall, Jodi O'Brien, Aaron Panofsky, Jason Patch, Caroline Persell, Richard Peterson, Liss Platt, Shannon Reed, Susan Rosenbloom, Tchad Sanger, Kristen Schilt, Karen Snedker, Jeremy Stolow, Jason Swierk, Brenda Vrkljan, and Michael Young. Support and encouragement may come in unexpected ways, and I was certainly pleased to happen on a group of blogging sociologists who have created an open and welcoming professional community that has inspired me to write early and often. Although this community has a growing and ever-changing cast of characters, I include particular thanks to Jeremy Freese of Scatterplot (scatter.wordpress.com), Kieran Healy of Crooked Timber (www.crookedtimber.org), Brayden King of orgtheory.net (orgtheory.wordpress.com), Alan Schussman (schussman.com), Chris Uggen (chrisuggen.blogspot.com), and Drek the Uninteresting of Total Drek (totaldrek.blogspot.com).

I am especially lucky to be friends with a great number of amazing women. These strong, smart, funny, and caring friends have helped me through the good days and bad. Several of them I have mentioned above, but I have to give special thanks to two friends without whose love and support I would not be who I am today. Over the many years of writing this book, my good friends Karen Albright and Carrie James gave me intellectual and emotional support in so many ways and with such deep love that it feels like I am standing on their shoulders. I hope they will let me stay up here forever.

Of course, this book could not have come to be if not for the decades of work by activists in both the lesbian and gay movement and the religious right. I hope I have captured their work as fairly and accurately as possible here. I am grateful for the work of the historians and archivists who have made the records of these groups available to researchers. I thank the ONE Institute in Los Angeles; the Human Sexuality Collection at Cornell University; the Lesbian Herstory Archives in Brooklyn, New York; the Gay, Lesbian, Bisexual, and Transgender Historical Society of Northern California in San Francisco; the International Gay Information Center at the New York Public Library; and the National Archive of Lesbian and Gay History in New York City. I am especially grateful to the activists who agreed to be interviewed for this book.

My editor, Jason Weidemann, has been a great resource as I revised the manuscript into a book, as have the editors of the Social Movements, Protest, and Contention series at the University of Minnesota Press: Bert Klandermans,

Ron R. Aminzade, David S. Meyer, and Verta Taylor. I am grateful for their encouragement, critical feedback, and advice.

Finally, I would like to thank my family for their love and support over the years as I worked on this project. Lane Dunlop, whose schedule leaves him exhausted yet whose support has been tireless, did everything under the sun to help me complete this book, not the least of which was selecting just the right music for every occasion. Our son, Maxwell James Fetner Dunlop, has provided endless sweetness and love, and I dedicate this book to him.

Introduction

October 1970. New York, New York. Dozens of radical lesbian and gay activists took over the offices of the publisher of *Harper's Magazine.* The magazine had just published an article about the gay lifestyle, claiming that homosexuality is an anathema. The author, Joseph Epstein, wrote "if I had the power to do so, I would wish homosexuality off the face of this earth" (1970, 51). The protesters served breakfast pastries and coffee to the office workers, introducing themselves as homosexuals. They met with the editors, shook the hands of secretaries and receptionists, and sang folk songs. By the end of the day, they felt they had "liberated" *Harper's* (Bell 1971, 131–37). Activists held a number of these liberation events over the years, convincing some newspapers to paint homosexuality in a more realistic light, encouraging businesses to adopt non-discriminatory hiring practices, and even passing a few pieces of gay rights legislation in some cities and counties across the nation.

At this early date, the lesbian and gay movement was small but vibrant. It was growing dramatically, with young adults inspired by the civil rights movement and the women's movement joining organizations started by older gay men and lesbian women, as well as starting their own new groups. Many of the public demonstrations, such as the liberation of *Harper's,* had a particular flair derived from the campy side of gay culture. While this form of protest might seem a bit fanciful, the movement had specific political and cultural goals, and it chose its targets strategically. Other early targets included the New York City Council, where legislation was repeatedly proposed to protect lesbians and gay men from employment and housing discrimination. The San Francisco Police Department was another important target, as a group of gay bar owners formed the Tavern Guild to put pressure on the city to rein in police harassment of their customers. The media, especially the Hollywood film industry and entertainment magazines, were also targeted by lesbian and gay movement activists, who were concerned with the portrayal of gay men and lesbians as either suicidal or as homicidal maniacs, if they were portrayed at all.

Throughout the early 1970s the lesbian and gay movement continued to grow and to contribute to some social change. This most often took the form of anti-discrimination law at a handful of municipalities and non-discrimination policies adopted by corporate human resource offices and university admissions statements. Urban enclaves and subcultural gay and lesbian communities continued to thrive and expand during this time. Gay-owned businesses began popping up in metropolitan areas, including lesbian and gay bookstores, gift shops, and community centers. At the same time, lesbian and gay communities in smaller cities and towns began to take root, often expanding from a single gay bar into a set of community institutions and social movement organizations. Lesbian and gay student groups sprouted up on college campuses across the country, and professional academics began to come out of the closet and discuss working conditions for lesbian and gay professors and graduate students, the choice of lesbian and gay research topics, and the role of academia in setting political agendas (see, for example, Crew 1978).

This diverse and growing social movement also experienced serious setbacks and barriers to social change. For example, lesbian and gay movement activists had trouble getting any coverage in the newspapers for their protests and legislative battles. They had difficulties reaching out to lesbian and gay people who did not live in larger towns and cities. Gay men and lesbians were still subject to criminalization for patronizing gay and lesbian bars and clubs, as well as for gender deviations such as dressing in drag or adopting a "butch" style of fashion. Relatively few media outlets featured portrayals of lesbian and gay people in a positive or even a neutral light, and politicians felt quite comfortable ignoring their legislative agendas. For better or for worse, all of this changed for the lesbian and gay movement in 1977 with the emergence of the anti-gay countermovement that would evolve into what is known today as the religious right.

January 1977. Dade County, Florida. Anita Bryant, a former beauty queen, singer, and television celebrity famous for promoting Florida orange juice, started to make a name for herself in a new way: as the leader of an anti-gay countermovement that started locally, in Dade County, Florida, and then spread across the country. Bryant was a friend of Phyllis Schlafly, the leader of the Eagle Forum, a conservative women's group that successfully organized against the passage of the Equal Rights Amendment. Bryant saw firsthand how social movement mobilization could work for conservative agendas as well as liberal ones (Bull and Gallagher 1996, 17). When she was approached by members of her church to make an appeal to the county commissioners to vote against legislation providing protection from discrimination for lesbian and gay people in the county, Bryant agreed (Bryant 1977, 14–18). When this did not work, Bryant founded a social movement group, named Save Our Children, and launched an initiative campaign to repeal the bill. Working mostly with other women from her church, Bryant gathered a team of volunteers to collect signatures on petitions. She appeared on Pat Robertson's televangelist show, *The 700 Club,* and claimed that gay men are child molesters trying to get jobs in schools and day care programs for easy access to young boys. As she says in her autobiography, "homosexuals cannot reproduce—so they must recruit. And to freshen their ranks, they must recruit the youth of America" (Bryant 1977, 87). Bryant's group successfully secured enough signatures to put a repeal initiative on the ballot, and the measure passed overwhelmingly at the next election, keeping gay rights out of Miami–Dade County for decades.

This local success encouraged Bryant to expand her activism, and she organized a tour around the country, teaching people how to form local organizations and use the ballot initiative process to repeal gay rights ordinances. Using church networks, Bryant found many conservative Christian women and men who were also outraged at the marginal gains of the lesbian and gay movement and wanted to do something about it. Bryant wrote two books (Bryant 1977; Bryant and Green 1978), and her group held rallies, distributed information, and provided seed money and organizational advice to Christians interested in opposing lesbian and gay rights measures across the country. Her organization helped set up several local groups to challenge gay rights ordinances. Bryant's fledgling social movement successfully repealed four anti-discrimination bills across the country, losing only one of the initiatives it managed to put on the ballot (Button, Rienzo, and Wald 1997, 69).

With Bryant's swift nationwide campaign to undo years of activism by the lesbian and gay movement, a new era was born. Right-wing activism such as Anita Bryant's petition drives and Phyllis Schlafly's anti-ERA activism evolved over the next few years into the Moral Majority. Evangelical Christianity and biblical literalism moved from the margins of political discourse to the center, integrating effectively with the Republican Party in the late 1980s. The religious right, as it became known, developed into a major, multitiered political force. Political insiders had the ear of politicians at every level (and, in many cases, became office holders themselves). Organizational leaders managed major Christian media outlets, including television networks, radio stations, book and magazine publishers, and school and home-schooling curriculums. Church networks were developed to effectively disseminate information on political activism and voting recommendations. At the local level, kitchen campaigns, in which women wrote letters to their representatives regarding issues determined by those at the top, gave the movement the appearance of a grassroots effort, while holding on to the organizationally efficient model of top-down decision making.

The religious right has proven a very powerful political force. Its multi-issue platform extends well beyond lesbian and gay rights issues, and its impact is felt by a wide variety of activists working toward progressive social change. However, along with its anti-abortion stance, anti-gay activism forms the core of this movement's platform. Over time, the religious right's attention to anti-gay issues has waxed and waned, but the lesbian and gay movement has never been out of its sights. Sexual morality is at the core of the religious right's agenda, although its platform includes other issues, such as school prayer, welfare reform, and restricted sex education in schools. Like abortion, homosexuality has proven a lucrative fundraiser, sparking outrage and garnering donations from constituents (Berlet 1998, 262–67).

At the point when Anita Bryant started her petition drive, lesbian and gay activism experienced a sea change. No longer would lesbian and gay activists fight to get issues relating to homosexuality into the news. Now, for better or worse, they were a top story around the nation. And from this point on, lesbian and gay activists would have to do their work in an antagonistic dialogue with the religious right. Never again would activists be able to focus exclusively on how state legislators would respond to their petitions or on how open various corporations would be to including gay-friendly policies in their human resources statements. They would also have to consider what impact a counterprotest to their actions might have on their goals. This new worry changed the very nature of lesbian and gay activism.

As the young, anti-gay countermovement matured and grew into the Moral Majority and then the religious right, the lesbian and gay movement became dwarfed by its opposing movement. The size of the religious right, whether measured in membership, size of organizations, revenue, or other resources, was dramatically greater than that of the lesbian and gay movement. If opposing movement activism were a head-to-head battle of strength, the religious right would have crushed the lesbian and gay movement outright. However, not only did both of these movements continue over the next three decades, they both grew in size and influence. It was only after the emergence of an anti-gay movement that the lesbian and gay movement grew into a large-scale, national social movement.

This book tells the story of these two opposing movements over time. As the history unfolds, it will become clear that the religious right has influenced the lesbian and gay movement on a number of levels. It has affected lesbian and gay activists' choices of which issues to rally around and which issues to put on the back burner. It has blocked or reversed the implementation of policies that would benefit lesbians and gay men. The religious right has changed the rhetoric that lesbian and gay activists use to express their claims. It has also influenced the choice of tactics by the lesbian and gay movement, and even the size and shape of many organizations within the movement. And perhaps most importantly, it has limited the lesbian and gay movement's ability to frame the public debate about gay rights. However, at the same time, the dynamics between opposing movements have propelled both of these movements forward in some ways, pushing issues of lesbian and gay rights into the political sphere, rallying support from individuals on both sides of the issue, and increasing memberships and budgets of movement organizations on each side of the issue. As this book lays out the history of one major pair of opposing movements, examining in particular the influence of the religious right on the lesbian and gay movement, it establishes some building blocks for a theoretical account of how opposing movements influence each other in general. Of course, in doing so, it also relies on a body of scholarship on social movements in general and opposing movements in particular. I provide a very brief overview below.

Opposing Movements: A Sociological Perspective

Sociologists have long endeavored to understand just how the world changes—how the collective will of people can sometimes make a significant shift in the social and political institutions of a nation and at other times have very little impact. Those who study social movements have chronicled grassroots activism and categorized many of the requisite pieces of the puzzle for activists to make social change: for example, resources, a favorable political context, the right connections to those with power, a cohesive collective identity, and a way to capture the problem that resonates with various audiences (see, for example, Amenta 2006; Amenta, Carruthers, and Zylan 1992; McCarthy and Zald 1977; Gamson 1975; McAdam 1982; Tarrow 1994). Social movement theorists have laid the groundwork for new studies to look deeper into the processes of activism and the problems that inevitably arise for activists in the long term, including political, cultural, and emotional factors.

Some social movement scholars have begun to address the additional issues up for consideration in the case of two movements fighting against each other, called opposing movements (see, for example, Andrews 2002; Lo 1982; Meyer and Staggenborg 1996, 1998; Rohlinger 2002). Many of these works consider what it is that makes opposing movements different from other social movements, what new questions they introduce to social movement scholarship, and what new puzzles they bring to activists themselves. By definition, social movements face a lot of opposition even when they do not encounter an opposing movement. Social movement groups comprise outsiders with limited access to the political system where decisions on social policy are made (Tilly 1978, 52). In many cases, they represent socially marginalized populations and small minorities who struggle to be recognized in a majority-rule, democratic society. They often face opposition from the state, from mainstream news media who ignore their claims, from religious organizations that are invested in the status quo, and from an uninterested public that is unfamiliar with the issues the movement is trying to raise. An opposing movement, whose goal is to derail the original social movement, produces a whole set of new problems and issues for movement activists to deal with. Social movements need to change the way they do their activism when an opposing movement joins the political arena. That an opponent is a social movement creates a dynamic that is unlike other forms of opposition.

Zald and Useem (1987), for example, claim that the relationship between opposing movements is dynamic and interactive. They describe this interactive, oppositional relationship as "loosely coupled conflict," arguing that victories allow movements to relax and have a demobilizing effect, but at the same time they inspire and mobilize the opposing movement into renewed action. Meyer and Staggenborg (1998) argue that opposing movements create opportunities for each other with their actions, claims, tactics, and frames for activism by altering the political terrain in which social movement actors are accustomed to working. Social movement organizations choose strategies, frame political claims, and develop protest tactics they believe will be appropriate to the political context, effective for accomplishing their goals, and consistent with their organizational values (Meyer and Staggenborg 1996). Opposing movements, by shifting political venues, disputing social movement claims, lobbying politicians, and introducing new frames, alter the political context and create new problems for activists, as well as new opportunities.

This book builds on this scholarship by examining in detail the historical influence of one movement, the religious right, on another, the lesbian and gay movement. I focus on the impact of one opposing movement on another in order to maintain a clear purpose. By keeping its sights on the responses that various individuals and organizations in the lesbian and gay movement have made over the last few decades, this book isolates the impact of one movement on the other. Of course, like other scholars of opposing movements, I expect each of these movements to influence the other in a dynamic set of relations. To study how these influences work, however, takes our attention away from the vast discrepancy in size and resources between these two movements. For example, Zald and Useem's description (1987) of patterns of mobilization and demobilization cannot account for the different opportunities and constraints facing activists in each of these movements. The selection of cases here will add to the scholarship on opposing movements by paying close attention to this factor.

The lesbian and gay movement's survival—indeed, its dramatic growth and vibrancy in light of such strong opposition as the religious right—is an interesting story in its own right. These two movements have together brought a nation's attention to an issue that, not forty years ago, was relegated to the margins of society. Public opinion on homosexuality and lesbian and gay rights has shifted dramatically in these decades, and the policy battles of these opposing movements have been, and continue to be, at the forefront of American political discourse (Yang 1997). In analyzing these dynamic, long-term opposing movements this book focuses on seven mechanisms through which the religious right has made an impact on the activism of the lesbian and gay movement: (1) the impact on the rhetoric and framing used by the lesbian and gay movement; (2) the religious right's effect on the lesbian and gay movement's mobilization of resources over time; (3) the religious right's influence on the organizational forms of lesbian and gay movement groups as it pushed anti-gay activism into various political venues; (4) the evocation of lesbian and gay movement activists' emotions; (5) the religious right's role in selecting the issues on which the lesbian and gay movement targeted its activism; (6) the religious right's ability to impede political and legislative progress; and (7) the religious right's ability to draw public attention to lesbian and gay movement issues. The book is organized more or less chronologically as well as according to these mechanisms. Toward the end of the book, I take a step back to evaluate the changes in public opinion toward homosexuality and lesbian and gay rights over this historic battle that has been famously dubbed the "culture war" (Buchanan 1992, 2544).

To assemble this historical account, I rely on many primary and secondary data sources. Historical accounts and sociological analyses of the lesbian and gay movement, the religious right, and evangelical Christian communities form the basis for much of the history presented here. News accounts from mainstream as well as lesbian and gay and Christian media provide an important supplementary source of information, as do memoirs of activists in each of these movements. Organizational histories and other records, mostly from lesbian and gay movement organizations, but including some records from groups in the religious right, have been pivotal in revealing the internal decision-making processes of these social movements. I am indebted to the various lesbian and gay archives that have preserved these organizational records, as well as the myriad flyers, newsletters, press releases, and other communiqués that form the basis of my analysis in chapter 2. These include the Human Sexuality Collection at Cornell University; the Lesbian Herstory Archives in Brooklyn; the Gay, Lesbian, Bisexual, and Transgender Historical Society of Northern California in San Francisco; the online collection of the ONE Institute National Gay and Lesbian Archives in Los Angeles; the International Gay Information Center at the New York Public Library; and the National Archive of Lesbian and Gay History in New York City. Finally, interviews with seven leaders and past leaders of lesbian and gay movement organizations across the country round out this analysis, as they provide their perspective on the delicate balance of decision making in the face of a powerful opposing movement.

Terminology

Settling on a terminology to use for each of these movements is a particular challenge. There is no term that addresses either of these movements in a historically accurate way throughout the period covered here. Even within a particular era, the identity of the movement was often in dispute, with some organizations using different terminology from others. The terms I have chosen, the lesbian and gay movement and the religious right, are imperfect. The term "lesbian and gay movement" would not accurately describe, for example, the homophile activists of the 1960s and '70s, a time before "lesbian and gay" caught on among activists. Further, it is at once too inclusive and too exclusive. It implies that gay men's activism was ever collaborating with lesbian women's activism, which was certainly not the case in many points over this movement's history. It also leaves out people who have made important contributions to the movement, especially bisexual, transsexual, and transgender activists. To use the contemporary term "LGBT movement" for a historical account, however, would be to give too much credit for inclusion to a movement that even today makes gender identity and bisexuality low priority issues overall. The term "religious right" is a controversial one as well, given that the social movement organizations this term describes would not use this term to identify themselves. However, I use this term to make clear the connections between the lobbying and think-tank organizations that have come to be known as the New Christian Right and the activist organizations that call themselves the pro-family movement. These are densely networked organizations that share an overarching agenda, tactics, and resources. I consider them to be a single social movement, and while some have criticized the term "religious right" for implying more connections to non-evangelical religious conservatives than may be deserved, I think it is the most appropriate term for the purposes of this analysis.

A Note on My Perspective

Researchers of social movements often find themselves struggling to situate themselves vis-à-vis the movements they study. Kathleen Blee (2002, 60–61) notes how difficult this becomes in the extreme situation of violent groups whose values are objectionable to the researcher. Even among nonviolent groups, this can be a challenge. In the case of opposing movements, activists reasonably want to know which side you are on. Arlene Stein's discussion (2001, 229–32) of how she managed her interactions with people engaged in anti-gay activism was influential to my own decisions of how to present myself to activists. Stein's identity as a Jewish lesbian placed her in opposition to the anti-gay activists in Oregon, and she was honest without disclosing her identity until someone asked. In my case, my social identity (as a white, straight woman) was not so easy for activists to read. Most activists chose not to ask about my sexual identity. Instead, they turned to my credentials to check out my social location and my political leanings. Getting a Ph.D. in sociology from New York University, for example, meant that activists in each opposing movement read my political ideology (correctly) as liberal, and this meant that I had much better access to lesbian and gay movement leaders than to those in the religious right. My distance from the religious right was exacerbated by my lack of religious affiliation; I could not talk to these activists as a fellow Christian, which made it difficult to establish trust. When I did get a few interviews with religious right activists, most spent little time answering the questions I put to them about strategy and decision making, focusing instead on trying to convince me of the value of their anti-gay stance. Although my politics do come down on the side of the lesbian and gay movement, I endeavored to be even-handed in collecting data for this project, as well as in the writing of this book. As much as I acknowledge that the social location of every researcher matters, the goal of the book is not to pick sides between these opposing movements, but to examine the dynamics of opposition itself. I hope I do that with as little bias as possible.

An Overview of the Book

In chapter 1, I document the social contexts from which each of these movements emerged. For the religious right, this entails an examination of the growth of fundamentalist and neo-evangelical Christianity in the United States. Ironically, it was the Christian evangelical community's withdrawal from the secular world that created the very conditions that would make it so successful as a politically oriented social movement in later decades. Christian evangelicals engaged in extensive institution building throughout the middle of the twentieth century in order to avoid interaction with what they saw as the immorality of modern life, creating alternative education systems, media outlets, and, of course, church networks. These institutions established a strong infrastructure for a burgeoning social movement in the 1970s. In the case of the lesbian and gay movement, I point to the role, well documented elsewhere, that the social upheaval of World War II played in the growth of lesbian and gay communities in port cities around the United States. I then discuss the early years of the lesbian and gay movement, before the anti-gay opposing movement emerged.

In chapter 2, I look closely at the historical moment when the Christian anti-gay movement emerged and captured national attention. Anita Bryant, using her wholesome image as a beauty queen, singer, and mother, appealed to people's traditional morality in her crusade against gay rights. Though Bryant claimed that she did not reject homosexual people, she regularly claimed that their goal was to use gay rights legislation to gain better access to children in order to molest them. The emergence of this social movement provides an important window into the dynamics of opposing movements as a point of comparison between the actions of the lesbian and gay movement prior to the Christian anti-gay movement's emergence, and the choices they made immediately following. Chapter 2 examines the way that lesbian and gay movement activists working on different issues responded to the emergence of this opposing movement and how they tried to turn this opposition into an advantage.

Chapter 3 considers the organizational development of these movements as they grew and evolved through the 1980s. For the Christian anti-gay movement, this meant the dissolution of local anti-gay organizations and the emergence of a national, multi-issue Christian conservative movement, the Moral Majority. Though short-lived as an organization, the Moral Majority set the stage for the ongoing development of the religious right, establishing network ties, promoting a multi-issue agenda, and establishing the political currency of a conservative Christian collective identity. For the lesbian and gay movement, the AIDS crisis took its deadly toll on gay men throughout the country, and the lack of help from the conservative Reagan government forced gay communities to build institutions to provide services, education, and even health care to its afflicted members. As the decade continued, the presence of a highly centralized, national opposing movement created pressure for the lesbian and gay movement to dedicate resources to larger, national organizations. Given the success of many AIDS organizations, there was increased support among lesbian and gay movement activists and constituents for this organizational model.

By the end of the 1980s the religious right had begun to acquire some power within the Republican Party at both the state and national levels. The lesbian and gay movement pursued a similar strategy to make inroads to the Democratic Party, but with more mixed results. Chapter 4 considers how the religious right pulled the lesbian and gay movement into party politics, a move that proved to be more of a distraction than a benefit for lesbian and gay activism. An ambivalent Democratic Party turned out to be only a weak ally of the lesbian and gay movement. Even when Democrats assumed control of the presidency in 1992, the Clinton administration failed to overturn the military's ban of gay men and lesbians, and although it proposed a federal gay rights bill, the Employment Non-Discrimination Act, it was unable to secure its passage. In this same period, however, the Republican Party, supported by its now fully integrated partners in the religious right, partnered with Clinton to pass the Defense of Marriage Act, a bill intended to confirm the exclusion of same-sex couples from the institution of marriage.

For most of the course of the histories of these two opposing movements, there was little on-the-ground contact between protestors from each side. This is in stark contrast with, for example, the pro-choice and pro-life movements, in which protests and counterprotests occur regularly outside women's health clinics. For these two movements, however, a renewal of Anita Bryant's ballot initiative tactic in the early 1990s resulted in street marches, rallies, and gatherings of both sides over anti–gay rights legislation proposed in Oregon, Colorado, and Cincinnati, Ohio. Newspaper editorials, talk radio shows, churches, and bookstores became sites of gay rights debate. Focusing in on these hotly contested initiatives, each of which sought to ban gay rights legislation in their respective locales, chapter 5 examines the interactive aspects of activists' strategies, as well as the power of one movement to force the other to work on one issue in its agenda to the neglect of others it may find more important.

Chapter 6 examines the activism of the late 1990s and the beginning years of the twenty-first century. First, through the religious right's direct attack on lesbian and gay identity itself: sexual conversion therapy. The "ex-gay" strategy was an attempt to convince mainstream America that homosexuality is a choice, one that can be undone through "sexual conversion" therapy. Testimonials of "ex-gay" men and "former lesbians" were the mainstay of this campaign, a strategy that turned embarrassing for the movement when several prominent ex-gay leaders slipped back into their old homosexual habits. The analysis then turns to the fiercest battle between the religious right and the lesbian and gay movement thus far: same-sex marriage. A few pro-gay actions in the form of court decisions in Vermont and Massachusetts, as well as high-profile civil disobedience in San Francisco, have been dwarfed by the current political climate of the Bush administration, which claims to support an amendment to the U.S. Constitution to ban same-sex marriage altogether (although it has not proposed such an amendment). As these issues continue to be fought out, I consider the impact that each of these movements has had on popular attitudes toward homosexuality and lesbian and gay rights. Poll data suggest that the religious right has not had a negative impact on attitudes toward homosexuality; in fact, the American people are becoming more tolerant of lesbians and gay men at a rapid pace.

In chapter 7, I return to the more general issue of how an opposing movement can change the course of a social movement. I use the case of the religious right and the lesbian and gay movement to highlight the unique difficulties of opposing movements, and to develop an understanding of the oppositional, yet symbiotic, relationships that opposing movements develop over time. I consider aspects of activism such as the forms of social movement organizations, the issues that social movements choose to work on at any given time, the frames and the language that social movements use, and the emotional dynamics of opposing movements. I also consider the varying degrees to which different social movement organizations will choose to engage the opposing movement. While some organizations feel compelled to respond to every statement and action of their opposing movement, others largely ignore the opponent as they map out the course of their activism.

This historical overview of the actions and reactions of these two movements reveals a dynamic relationship in which each side works against the other, and yet each benefits in some ways from the activism of the other. The religious right, with its vast resources and political power, has turned a spotlight onto lesbian and gay rights issues, helping the lesbian and gay movement get its message to a wide public audience. Similarly, the religious right has helped push these issues into the platforms of political parties and elected officials. It is not surprising that the rich and powerful religious right has introduced serious barriers to policy change and effectively clawed back some of the gains of the lesbian and gay movement. However, despite this opposition, the lesbian and gay movement has continued its activism, growing rather than shrinking in the face of the religious right.

1

The Roots of Activism:
Homosexuals and Christian Evangelicals before the Fight

We, the Androgynes of the world, have formed this responsible corporate body to demonstrate by our efforts that our physiological and psychological handicaps need be no deterrent in integrating 10 percent of the world's population towards the constructive social progress of mankind.
—Mattachine Society manifesto, 1953

If we had more hell in the pulpit, we would have less hell in the pew.
Billy Graham, 1964

In the 1950s and 1960s the worlds of homosexuals and Christian evangelicals could not have been further apart. Neither of these groups had much of a presence in the political sphere, yet this era was a critical period in which the ideological and structural foundations of each of these movements were laid. Through much of the middle of the century, Christian evangelicals were dedicated to withdrawal not only from politics but from the secular world more generally, as they perceived it to be filled with harmful, immoral influences. From the 1930s through the 1960s, evangelical Christians were dedicated to building alternative social networks and religious and educational institutions as shields from the cultural influences of the outside world (Diamond 1995, 92–106). Many Christian evangelicals thought that popular music was a particularly evil influence on children, as was the sexual content of magazines, films, and television. Public schools presented material that contradicted biblical literalism; evolution was a particular point of contention. In response, evangelical Christians retreated from the secular world, built institutions that supported their own values and ideology, and encouraged their loved ones to act in a way that would make them worthy of salvation. Perhaps ironically, it is exactly this retreat by Christian evangelicals from the secular world that laid the groundwork for their later emergence in both grassroots political activism and party politics. The development of church networks, bible institutes, religious retreats, television and radio networks, videos, and a host of children's books, bible study pamphlets, and so on, became the backbone of the Christian anti-gay movement of the 1970s, as well as the larger political movement, the religious right. This included not only a dense network of affiliated organizations but also a strongly held ideology of shared Christian values and a distinctive Christian identity that positioned true Christians as outside of the political and social mainstream (for details, see Smith et al. 1998; Wilcox 1992). Evangelical Christians had amassed considerable financial resources and membership numbers as they created wide informational networks and an ideological consistency among their members (Diamond 1998).

Though lesbians and gay men were similarly sequestered from mainstream culture, this was due more to oppression than to a separatist ideology. In the 1950s and early '60s, the bar scenes in urban enclaves that developed after World War II fostered gay and lesbian cultures that were more or less hidden from the view of the straight world. These social settings were subject to surveillance and random raids by police. On the streets, men who acted too feminine and women who appeared too manly risked harassment and violence. The McCarthy era of the early to mid-1950s was a particularly oppressive historical moment for lesbians and gay men, as the federal government added to the culture of oppression by claiming that homosexuals were perverts who posed a communist threat (D'Emilio 1983, 41–43). Under McCarthyism, the federal government fired hundreds of homosexual men and women from bureaucratic jobs and dishonorably discharged many others from the military (D'Emilio 1983, 44–45). Despite these serious threats, gay men and lesbians managed to create some scattered social movement groups. Activists published newsletters, held social events, and sponsored some protests of police entrapment and harassment. Some trailblazers took McCarthy's policies on directly, forming picket lines in Washington, D.C., to protest the purge of homosexuals from federal jobs.

Although these communities were developing in very separate social spheres, together these early activities provided the building blocks of the activism that later became entrenched opposing movements. On each side, actors formed cohesive group identities, identified key grievances, and built social networks that were critical to the grassroots activism of the late 1960s and the 1970s. However, though the processes were similar, the size of these efforts were markedly different, with the Christian evangelical community operating on a much larger scale than the homophile groups. This difference in scale would persist throughout the history of these opposing movements.

Christian Activism in the Secular World

Although the lesbian and the gay movement and the Christian anti-gay movement crossed paths in the mid-1970s and have remained intertwined ever since, the two movements have distinctly unrelated histories. While gay activist history in the United States reaches back only fifty years or so, the roots of conservative Christian activists are much deeper. The Christian anti-gay movement did not spring up out of the blue in 1977. Rather, the movement was born out of a dense set of networks and a distinct ideology and collective identity that were the products of decades of institution building by Christian evangelicals. These church networks, publication industries, and educational institutions were important foundations for the activism of the religious right toward the end of the century.

Retreat from the Modern World

At one point in the history of the United States, the story of Christian evangelicalism was the story of the nation. The dominance that Protestant evangelicals enjoyed crossed the realms of politics, church, and education (Oldfield 1996, 14–15). Drawing from Protestant roots of the colonial era, Christian evangelicals' position of cultural and religious dominance lasted through the nineteenth century (Marsden 1980, 11). As is the privilege of dominant groups, Protestant evangelicals could claim the United States to be a Christian nation, despite the religious diversity of more marginalized clusters of Asian, African, Native American, and Eastern and Southern European citizens and residents.

In the early decades of the twentieth century, however, this synchronicity between Protestantism and American identity changed drastically. Changes in the modern world created schisms within Protestant churches. Inside the church, biblical criticism and liberal theologies began to challenge orthodoxies. In the secular world, the scientific community began to reject the integration of biblical teachings with scientific theory. Scientific advances such as Darwinian evolution challenged a literal interpretation of the Bible. And sweeping demographic changes in America, such as the influx of Catholic and Jewish immigrants from Ireland and from Southern and Eastern Europe, pushed diverse religious views into American life. While mainline Protestant denominations generally adapted to this changing world, moving away from biblical literalism and embracing scientific discovery, some conservative Protestants decided to fight these changes both in the church and in secular society. Around the turn of the century, these resisters became known as fundamentalists, owing to a tract that they produced, titled *The Fundamentals* (Smith et al. 1998, 6). After efforts to displace the liberal leadership from Protestant churches failed, and with the debacle of the Scopes Monkey Trial in 1925, these fundamentalists decided to break off from mainline Protestantism and form their own churches.

This separation from Protestant denominations was accompanied by a larger retreat from the secular world as well. Fundamentalists in this era were so emphatic about doctrinal purity that they rejected not only liberal theology but association with anyone who subscribed to such theology. This led to rather extreme efforts at isolation from other Protestant denominations, as well as from the larger society. As sociologist Christian Smith observes, "The total effect [of this retreat] was powerful and conspicuous. By the end of the 1930s, much of conservative Protestantism—under the banner of fundamentalism—had evolved into a somewhat reclusive and defensive version of its nineteenth century self" (Smith et al. 1998, 9). At this time, there was a proliferation of independent fundamentalist churches. It would be inaccurate to represent fundamentalist Protestantism in this era (up to the current day) as a denomination. Rather, fundamentalism as a set of principles guided numerous independent churches that belonged to no denomination. Fundamentalists' obsession with doctrinal purity, combined with the principles of isolation from those with whom a church has doctrinal disagreements, led to innumerable stand-alone, neighborhood non-denominational churches. Fundamentalism is a term that is used to describe these various independent churches, as well as others that claim denominational ties but still self-identify as Christian fundamentalist.

However, not all fundamentalists thought that isolationism was the best choice for conservative Protestants. These people believed that an obsession with doctrinal purity was causing fundamentalists to neglect their obligation to minister the word of God to the world. In the 1940s a group of reformers, calling themselves neo-evangelicals, mobilized like-minded Protestants and created a national network of churches that retained an orthodox theology while committing to building communities separate from the secular world. This resulted in the establishment of the National Association of Evangelicals, a network that included evangelical churches as well as Pentecostals, charismatics, and other non-fundamentalist churches.

Building Christian Evangelical Networks

The neo-evangelicals made a break from fundamentalists, refusing to retreat from social and political life. However, they still shared fundamentalists' distrust of corrupting secular influences. This development led the Christian evangelical community to build a vast expanse of institutional supports for the communication of evangelical ideology, community, and identity. One important branch of this institutionalization was the development of networks such as the National Association of Evangelicals, which embraced evangelical-leaning churches from a variety of denominations as well as from non-denominational churches. Similar network organizations were found in denominational affiliations, such as the Independent Fundamental Churches of America, the Orthodox Presbyterian Church, the General Association of Regular Baptist Churches, the Bible Presbyterian Church, and the Fundamentalist Baptist Fellowship (Carpenter 1997, 45–49). These denominational networks provided a variety of institutional supports for churches, similar to the ways that mainline Protestant denominations supported their members.

Evangelical leaders sought to reach out to these congregations as well as to the masses. Over several decades, a number of Christian evangelicals created a wide variety of para-church organizations that were not tied to any denomination. The size and scope of these organizations is unique to the evangelical Christian community. Many scholars have noted that they provide services and information to far more people than do denominational organizations (Smith et al. 1998, 9–13). For example, evangelical Christians have established a number of educational institutions: bible institutes, liberal arts colleges, and summer bible camps for children and young adults. Youth ministries provide after-school evangelical education, summer activities, and Sunday school events. A number of evangelistic, missionary agencies have been established around the world, providing both young people and entire families with opportunities to travel as missionaries. Most of these institutions are self-sustaining, for-profit ventures. Because they are not limited by denomination, they can and do provide services to a wide array of evangelical Christians, regardless of the doctrinal theology of their particular congregation. By emphasizing the commonalities among evangelical Christians in general, these para-church institutions have been vital in creating and sustaining a broadly defined Christian identity that is distinct from mainline Protestantism. Much of the work of this identity building has been accomplished through Christian evangelical media.

Christian Evangelical Media

The growth of Christian evangelical media began well before the televangelist boom of the 1970s and '80s. Perhaps the most important medium for Christian evangelicalism has been radio. The theatrical style of evangelical revivals made them perfect for radio, and evangelical Christians were among the pioneers of this new form of broadcasting (Diamond 1995, 97, 337n29). In the 1920s and '30s radio evangelism expanded dramatically; stations could be found anywhere in the country and at just about any time of day. The founding of the National Association of Evangelicals in 1947 included the establishment of an official radio arm, the National Religious Broadcasters. By 1983 the National Religious Broadcasters had over nine hundred radio station members. Richard Ostling (1984, 48) claims that daily and weekly radio shows are "probably still the backbone of evangelical broadcasting, complemented by largely or wholly religious radio stations."

Print media have also been important to the communication of evangelical Christian ideas. Christian book publishers, bookstores, newsletters, and magazines have been established both by denominational organizations and independently. The independent media organizations have often outpaced their denominational counterparts in terms of sales and readership. These include history, theological works, and popular fiction, as well as Sunday school curricula. The Christian Booksellers Association, founded in 1950, has 3,200 member stores.

Religious broadcasting was present early on in the days of television as well, but networks chose to give more air time to Catholic and mainline Protestant denominations. One notable exception to the exclusion of evangelical Christians was Billy Graham, whose popularity with the public gave him an early start in television broadcasting. Graham's show, *The Hour of Decision,* ran for three years in the early 1950s but did not make much of a splash. However, he returned to television in 1957 and remained a fixture of religious broadcasting for over forty years (Martin 1991). Most other televangelists (from whom Graham tried to distance himself) were not able to purchase airtime until 1960, when the FCC changed its policies about public interest programming (see Hadden and Shupe 1988 for a full discussion of this policy change). By the 1970s televangelism was thriving, with large audiences and high profits, and its growth did not slow down until several of the most prominent television preachers were embroiled in scandal. Despite the bad publicity that these scandals caused, televangelism carries on today, broadcasting to dozens of countries around the globe.

The Christian Family

The family is often viewed as a safe haven from a hostile world by conservative Christians who are suspicious of the influences of secular society. This idea of family became an important aspect of both Christian identity and, later, the political activism of the religious right. Myriad squabbles over doctrinal purity, and the belief that individuals could use common sense to understand the word of God, meant that church hierarchies did not have the ability to maintain a common doctrine to be passed down from one generation to the next. Instead, the family became the place where evangelical doctrine was taught to younger generations. Transmission of "family values" was the responsibility of parents to their children. For Christian evangelicals, this meant telling their children about the positive values they held and enforcing the strict behavioral norms that accompany a literal interpretation of the Bible, as well as preventing unwanted influences from entering their families' domain (Carpenter 1997, 61).

It was fairly common for evangelical families to forbid dancing and listening to popular music. Christian evangelicals were offended by educational material presented in public schools when it contradicted biblical literalism, such as evolution's challenge to creationism. Anti-communist ideology was also folded into these concerns about the secular world. Some of the most prominent evangelical leaders claimed that communist subversion of the nation was near. They taught their followers that communists had infiltrated the nation and were using sex and music to weaken and distract children. When the country was sufficiently decadent and self-absorbed, America would be unable to defend itself against communist attack, either from abroad or from within (Berlet and Lyons 2000, 201). Premillennialist ideology holds that these symptoms of moral decay are proof that the world as it stands is unsalvageable, and that the best work Christians can do is provide a safe, moral environment for their children, in order to ensure that their souls are saved.

To accomplish this, evangelical Christian families relied on their churches and on the para-church organizations that supported their own values and ideology; members of these institutions encouraged their loved ones to act in ways that would make them worthy of salvation, according to their beliefs. In premillennial dispensationalist prophecy, those who are true believers will experience rapture just prior to the apocalypse, after which Christ will reign on earth for one thousand years. All of the bodies of the truly faithful will be lifted off this earth in the dispensation, or rapture, and they will go to heaven. The non-believers will remain on earth and suffer greatly the famine, war, and vengeance of God before the new era of peace begins. This belief in dispensation encouraged the organization of the evangelical Christian world as a separate sphere through the middle of the century.

Much of the ideology communicated by the Christian media emphasized the importance of the Christian family. This ideal family consisted of married parents with children. It adhered not only to strict gender roles, but also to the missive that the wife should play the role of humble servant to the household and, more specifically, to the husband. Parents should be dedicated to the crafting of a strong moral character in their children, and the Christian institutions described above dedicated themselves to providing support for parents' efforts. The family became seen as a holy space, a sacrosanct institution in which the word of God could be best understood.

Christian Evangelical Identity

Over the course of the twentieth century, conservative evangelical Christians created and institutionalized a unique Christian identity. The combination of fundamentalists breaking away from the modern world and evangelicals building para-church organizations laid the groundwork for the Christian evangelical activism that emerged in the 1970s. Because fundamentalists were so scattered and divided about doctrinal interpretations, denominational affiliations dissolved. Instead, conservative Christians built an identity that embraced broad Christian principles and positioned itself in opposition to the immoral secular world. Evangelicals' retreat from the secular world, followed by expansive institution building, created bountiful resources that supported evangelical Christian families' efforts to live in alternative social spaces. These same resources were also very valuable in building a powerful social movement in the 1970s and '80s.

The development of church networks, bible institutes, religious retreats, and television and radio networks, as well as the development of a variety of Christian media products such as videos, children's books, and Bible study pamphlets, turned out to be the very elements that make up a strong social movement (McAdam 1982; McCarthy and Zald 1977; Walsh 1981). Together, these resulted in a solid organizational network and a distinctive Christian identity. This identity positioned true Christians as outsiders of the political and social mainstream, and it both encompassed and cemented a strongly held ideology of shared Christian values, such as a narrowly defined sexual morality, support for traditional gender hierarchies, and belief in the superiority of the male-headed, nuclear family (Apostolidis 2000, 9–11). Evangelical Christians had amassed impressive financial resources and membership numbers, and they had created wide informational networks and an ideological consistency among their members that would turn out to serve political ends very well (Diamond 1998, 172).

Christian Evangelical Entry into Secular Politics

Contrary to popular media accounts of the religious right, Christian evangelicals did not necessarily push their way into party politics as much as they were pulled. Key figures in conservative political circles in Washington report that they had to spend many meetings convincing evangelical Christian leaders such as Jerry Falwell, Pat Robertson, and James Kennedy that they should direct their resources, and their followers, to political participation (Oldfield 1996, 100–102). Fundamentalist leaders, such as Falwell, were concerned that their congregations and television audiences would reject them for failing to live up to their separatist principles. Others were wary of their followers' suspicion of the political system. However, while some criticism did befall these early political efforts, these leaders were largely supported for their activism. The development of the Moral Majority was a joint effort by political insiders, evangelical leaders, and socially conservative activists, and the group proved to Christian evangelists that their followers would not reject them if they entered the political arena. In fact, engaging in conflict with perceived enemies of morality would turn out to be a lucrative fund-raising device (Diamond 1989).

Just prior to the Moral Majority's introduction of Christian evangelicals into the political sphere, a few episodes of grassroots activism marked the entry of conservative Christian values into activist politics. Three conservative movements combined to form the vanguard of the religious right: the anti-feminist movement, the pro-life movement, and the anti-gay movement. Phyllis Schlafly began a successful campaign to prevent the passage of the Equal Rights Amendment and has continued to lead activists on various socially conservative issues (Diamond 1995, 167). The pro-life movement has been mobilized through various organizations since the *Roe v. Wade* ruling in 1973. Although opinion polls would indicate that evangelical Christians would support both of these issues, and indeed many evangelicals did join or donate to these groups, these were not necessarily Christian evangelical movements (Luker 1989, 196). Phyllis Schlafly herself is a conservative Catholic, and the pro-life movement is much too religiously diverse to characterize it as especially evangelical (Ginsburg 1989, 84–85). Where the connection to Christian evangelicals does lie is in the promotion of these activities through various evangelical Christian media sources, such as the Christian Broadcasting Network, various radio broadcasts, and through informal church networks (Diamond 1989).

It was in this political setting that Christian anti-gay activism emerged. The work of Schlafly's STOP ERA group looked like a promising sign that conservative activism in the form of social movements could be successful. But the larger political entry of Christian evangelicals that would eventually take the form of organizations like the Moral Majority, the Religious Roundtable, the Heritage Foundation, and the remaining infiltration of evangelical values into conservative politics captured by the term "religious right" had not yet coalesced (Himmelstein 1983, 24–25.). Like feminism and abortion rights activism, the lesbian and gay movement was disturbing to conservative Christians. The local, grassroots conservative Christian response that Anita Bryant started in Dade County, Florida in 1977, turned into what I call the Christian anti-gay movement as it continued to mobilize across the country after its initial political victory. Specifically evangelical Christian in its ideology, its rhetoric, its membership, and its leadership, the Christian anti-gay movement marked the entry of evangelical Christians into secular politics. As such, it provides an excellent case for the analysis of opposing movements. The next chapter will look at the first moment of the emergence of this opposing movement and analyze the impact that the Christian anti-gay movement had on the rhetorical strategies of the existing lesbian and gay movement activists.

The Lesbian and Gay Movement

In the United States, the lesbian and gay movement dates back to the 1950s. Elsewhere, however, political activism on behalf of homosexuals has a long and rich history. There has been much debate over the history of homosexuality, particularly in the West. It is clear that same-sex sexual activity has existed throughout many cultures and dates back at least as far as the written word (Greenberg 1988). However, some cultures also developed an understanding of homosexuality as an identity category, of the homosexual as a distinct type of person. Randolph Trumbach (1989, 130) makes the claim that, in European cities, homosexuals came to be understood to be a distinct type of people as early as the late seventeenth century. His historical work indicates that prior to this, same-sex acts between men did not necessarily indicate a preference for men, but rather a preference for sexual debauchery of various sorts. As market economies began to flourish, travel, trade, and the development of cities led to individual pursuits away from families of origin, and communities of men began to develop. In these communities, homosexually inclined individuals were able to find others who shared their interests in molly houses, "sociétés d'amour," public houses, and parks (Bray 1982; Norton 1992; Trumbach 1977). In England, in the late seventeenth and early eighteenth centuries same-sex behavior became associated with effeminacy. In response, male styles of dress and behavior became more masculinized, and norms against men kissing men or wearing garish clothing emerged (Trumbach 1989).

By the start of the nineteenth century a gay subculture was beginning to emerge in many countries in the West, evident in poetry and drama as well as in personal diaries and court records (Chauncey 1994; Greenberg 1988). While these public venues were male-oriented atmospheres, women also participated in same-sex relationships. The romantic era in England and the United States gave women social permission to express their feelings for close women friends. Romantic friendships developed between neighbors and friends, though they were not defined as sexual in a world that considered sexuality to be an exclusively male arena (Faderman 1981, 160). Such friendships were understood to be common, for example, in boarding schools for girls. For educated women, new opportunities to support themselves relieved them of some of the pressure to marry, and some "spinsters" were able to invent new careers in the helping professions that tended to be exclusively female. For example, settlement houses, where women could form long-term familial bonds with one another, became alternatives to patriarchal families (Smith-Rosenberg 1989). Many of these unmarried, educated women formed households with women partners, which were called "Boston marriages" on the East Coast. While it is not known whether these women were having sex with each other, diaries, letters, and personal papers make it clear that these were loving, romantic relationships (Faderman 1981). Communities of women-loving women were beginning to emerge by the end of the nineteenth century.

These expressions of same-sex intimacy did not immediately translate into activism on behalf of homosexuals. However, these early settings laid the foundation for future political activity. Over the course of the late nineteenth and early twentieth centuries a number of psychologists, psychoanalysts, and sexologists began to focus attention on people who were sexually attracted to those of their own sex. Sigmund Freud, Richard von Krafft-Ebing, and Havelock Ellis were particularly influential in redefining homosexuality as a psychological condition and those who experienced same-sex attraction as homosexual people, distinguishable from "normal" or "healthy" people by this trait (Katz 1995). This understanding of homosexuality influenced psychology for decades.

This particular definition of homosexuality as pathological opened up a new path of persecution for homosexual people. Rather than the extreme criminal punishments for sodomy, such as castration and death, which were very serious but seldom enforced, the medicalization of homosexuality meant that many more people would seek out or be forced to undergo a range of "treatments" to redirect their sexual appetites toward the opposite sex (Foucault 1978). These included institutionalization, shock therapy, induced vomiting, and talk therapy. On the other hand, as this same definition of homosexuality became widespread, doctors and lay people alike began to define the homosexual as a unique sort of person with particular traits, and the consensus over this definition was also an important prerequisite to the emergence of a social movement. Advocates of homosexual people emerged and tried to reform laws that served harsh punishments for sodomy and buggery (Greenberg 1988, 397–454). Among the best known of these earliest activists was Karl Ulrichs, a German lawyer who set the terms of the modern debate on homosexuality in the mid-nineteenth century by claiming that homosexuals should have equal treatment under the law (Adam 1995, 16–18).

Early forms of homosexual activism in Germany continued into the first part of the twentieth century, and several social movement organizations were established, including Magnus Hirschfeld's Scientific-Humanitarian Committee (Wissenschaftlich-Humanitäres Komitee) in 1897. These groups were destroyed under Hitler's reign, which by the end of the Holocaust had "effectively wiped away most of the early gay culture and its movement through systematic extermination and ideological control" (Adam 1995, 59). Gay clubs, coffee houses, and movement organizations were destroyed. Movement records were seized. Worst of all, thousands of homosexual men and women were taken to concentration camps, where many were killed (Plant 1986).

World War II

In the United States, World War II had quite a different effect on lesbian and gay subcultures. The social upheaval that accompanied the war meant that most young men joined the military, and many women supported the war effort by filling jobs in military support industries. Young adult women, mostly working class, left their hometowns in unprecedented numbers to move to the cities where factory jobs were available. Social norms shifted dramatically during the war. Working women who wore pants and cut their hair short were seen as patriotic citizens rather than social deviants (Frank, Ziebarth, and Field 1982; Weiss and Schiller 1988, 31–33). Overcrowded cities placed many women in single-sex living arrangements in overcrowded dormitories and apartments, and women of all marital statuses had the money and time to participate in a women's social scene at the end of the work day. In this setting, women could discover their sexual desires for other women and experiment with less risk of discovery by their families. Lesbian women had a better chance of meeting others like them. Other women joined the military, primarily the Women's Army Corps (WACS), which became an important institution for defining lesbian identity over the course of the war, creating a space for breaking down gender barriers and providing women-only social spaces within the military (D'Emilio 1983, 27–28).

In the military, men were also immersed in a gender-segregated lifestyle. While for the most part gay men were closeted within the military, many were persecuted by military officials and dishonorably discharged (Bérubé

1990, 139). However, in port cities where troops were on leave, men in uniform were a common sight in gay bars and cruising strips. During the war these cities where military personnel gathered were intensely crowded, and men often had to share beds in YMCAs or sleep in parks and movie theaters (D'Emilio 1983, 25). Among the many pressures that these large numbers of soldiers put on the cities was a demand for gay bars. This growth of the gay scene expanded existing gay subcultures significantly, outlasting the war and establishing many of the biggest gay enclaves today.

At the war's end, many gay men and lesbian women decided to settle down in these urban gay enclaves. Both discharged military personnel and women factory workers found themselves with more choices as to how their lives could proceed than had any previous generation. Separated from their families of origin and having supported themselves independently, many veterans of the war and the factories felt empowered to continue living on their own. While many lesbians and gay men moved back to their hometowns, others decided to live apart from their families and settle down in the developing "gay ghettos" (Levine 1979). Others moved beyond the port cities and participated in the smaller gay subcultures that were developing in such cities as Cleveland, Buffalo, and Denver (D'Emilio 1983, 32; Kennedy and Davis 1993). While norms for marriage and childrearing were strong for both men and women, in this postwar era there was a concerted effort sponsored by the U.S. federal government to encourage women in particular to return to their hometowns, settle into more traditional roles, and make their jobs available to men (Gluck 1987, 16–17). In this context, remaining single and living away from one's family of origin was not without social repercussions; however, this option was available to many more people than ever before.

McCarthy Era

Although urban gay enclaves created social spaces for lesbians and gay men and built a foundation for an emerging gay identity, these subcultures could not protect gay men and lesbians from persecution. The McCarthy era in the United States was a particularly oppressive historical moment for homosexuals. While this time is best remembered for the persecution of those alleged to be Communist Party members, McCarthy's task force, the House Un-American Activities Committee, included "sexual perverts" among those who were ferreted out, fired from government jobs, and stigmatized. McCarthyites used a twist of logic that held that homosexuals were a threat to the nation's security because, as sexual perverts, their low morals and marginal social status made them easy prey for communist spies. Thus, they were as good as spies themselves, and treated accordingly (Johnson 2004, 16).

Under McCarthy's watch, thousands of military personnel were dishonorably discharged and hundreds of civil servants were fired from the State Department (Johnson 2004, 15–39). This activity at the federal level encouraged local governments and police departments to step up their actions against gay bars and cruising strips. Private employers also conducted "loyalty-security" investigations that dug up evidence of homosexual conduct or affiliation. John D'Emilio (1983, 49) estimates that over 12 million employees faced such investigation during this time period. The FBI conducted intense surveillance of homosexual activity, collecting data on criminal and noncriminal activity in gay and lesbian subcultures.

Such a decidedly anti-homosexual stance by the federal government contributed to a cultural context in which police harassment of gays and lesbians escalated. Raids of gay bars and cruising strips increased, and arrests of gay men and lesbians surpassed one thousand annually in many cities (D'Emilio 1983, 49–51). Those arrested, regardless of whether charges were filed, often found their names, addresses, and places of employment printed in a local newspaper. Other forms of police intimidation included parking police cars outside gay bars and following patrons to their homes. Despite this intensely anti-gay social context, a few gay men and lesbians did manage to participate in grassroots activism. A handful of "homophile" groups, such as Mattachine and the Daughters of Bilitis, sprouted up around the country. These organizations published newsletters and held meetings where topics related to homosexuality were discussed in a formal setting. Many of these groups were very secretive, inviting only certain participants in these discussion groups to attend organizational and planning meetings.

Mattachine is widely credited with one of the first instances of grassroots political resistance, in the form of a criminal case of police entrapment of a homosexual man in 1952. According to Stuart Timmons's biography of Mattachine leader Harry Hay, an undercover police officer followed Dale Jennings from a gay bar to his home. When Jennings allowed the officer in and made some coffee, he found himself under arrest for "lewd and dissolute conduct." Many gay men had been unfairly persecuted in this manner, and the few attorneys who agreed to represent them typically recommended that they plead guilty, which would result in a fine rather than jail time. Harry Hay, one of Mattachine's founders, decided that this was the case that the group would fight. "I said, 'Look, we're going to make an issue of this thing. We'll say you are homosexual but neither lewd nor dissolute. And that cop is lying." The jury was deadlocked and the judge dismissed the charges. The Mattachine members were ecstatic and sent notices of the trial's outcome to many newspapers and radio and television stations, but none of them ran the story. However, the news of this case spread quickly through the gay community's underground networks, and Mattachine's membership grew quickly as a result (Timmons 1990, 164–68). As the group grew, it decided to distribute a newsletter to member chapters. The result was *ONE Magazine*, the first publication associated with gay activism in the United States. A remarkably polished publication, this magazine was printed throughout the 1950s and '60s. The postal authorities tried on a number of occasions to shut the publication down, but in 1958 the U.S. Supreme Court ruled that the post office must distribute the magazine (*One, Inc. v. Olesen*, 355 U.S. 371).

Throughout this early activist era, internal tensions mounted over whether the role of homophile organizations was to provide emotional support to homosexuals and create safe social places to gather, or to declare that homosexuality was not a sickness and to make demands on the state to end its harassment of gay men and women. Though the founders of Mattachine felt that political activism was urgently needed, in the hostile McCarthy era this path seemed too aggressive to many of the rank and file members. The group chose a more conservative path, electing new leaders and keeping a lower public profile. Other early organizations had similar internal disputes over organizational aims. For example, more conservative members of the Daughters of Bilitis wrested control of its publication, *The Ladder*, from Barbara Gittings, one of its more radical pioneers (Adam 1995, 77).

However, as the 1960s continued, the examples set by the civil rights movement, the New Left, antiwar activists, and Black Power separatists convinced many lesbian and gay men, and particularly younger activists, that more direct action should be taken. The voices arguing for political activism began to garner more attention and interest among members of these early organizations. Activists like Frank Kameny, who had been arguing for equal rights and full acceptance for homosexuals for years, began to inspire gay men and lesbians with his claim, "Gay is good!" By 1967 angry lesbian and gay voices could be heard calling for radical change. One Los Angeles protest of police brutality attracted several hundred homosexuals, and speakers at that rally called for aggressive, confrontational action (D'Emilio 1983, 227).

The Stonewall Rebellion

As Armstrong and Crage (2006) note, the 1969 Stonewall rebellion was not the first time a raid on a gay bar was met with resistance from patrons. Similar riots had broken out in San Francisco and Los Angeles before Stonewall. However, the fledgling movement did not have the resources to memorialize these riots. Over time, as the movement grew, it developed the capacity to commemorate the Stonewall riot with annual gay pride parades. This imprinted Stonewall as a watershed moment in lesbian and gay activist history. What began as spontaneous resistance to a routine police raid of the Stonewall Inn, a gay bar in New York City, developed into a rebellion that lasted three days. This protest caught the attention of the gay community in New York, and within a few days, a new protest group, the Gay Liberation Front (GLF), had called its first meeting (Adam 1995, 85). This ushered in the "gay liberation" era, which lasted from 1969 to about 1972. Though short lived, the high energy, creative tactics, and transformative ideology of gay liberation appealed to many members of the lesbian and gay community who had not previously been active, and memberships in activist organizations swelled (see Teal 1971). The gay liberation ideology held that social norms of sexuality should be subverted and eliminated. Not only should the norm of heterosexuality be undermined, but all sexual differences should be valued and embraced. Such a struggle would not only include political resistance against the state, its police, employers, landlords, and so on, but it would also require personal introspection and transformation in order to resist the repression that prevents gay potential within every human being from being expressed.

Like other liberation organizations in the United States during the late 1960s, gay liberation groups believed in creating alternative communities and social spaces to resist dominant power relations. Highly suspicious of the power associated with leadership, groups such as the GLF organized themselves as loosely and as nonhierarchically as possible. Issues were to be decided by the consensus that emerges out of friendly discussion, and meeting facilitators would rotate regularly so that everyone would have the same relationship to the group (Jay 1999, 80–82). There were to be no leaders and no followers. In addition, gay liberationists kept in mind the larger umbrella of oppression that affected women, Third World peoples, and poor people. Gay liberation organizations participated in civil rights protests and feminist marches, and they formed coalitions with other progressive groups. Members of the GLF were present at many of the rallies and protests for various causes, not only to support progressive politics, but also to make their cause known to other radicals and to form alliances (D'Emilio 1983, 233–39).

Gay liberation groups also made room for people who were not included by the existing homophile organizations. For example, transvestites who earned money hustling on the streets were integral members of early organizations such as the GLF. Women and men alike participated in the rotating leadership positions. However, new ideologies of creating nonsexist environments often gave way to individual habits, and women complained that they were being interrupted, dismissed, and overrun by the men in the group, who both outnumbered and out-shouted the women at many of the meetings. One woman activist, Karla Jay, would bring a softball bat to meetings when it was her turn to act as chair, hitting a pole in the center of the room to call the group to order. Jay claimed (1999, 125), "the bat was a great success; the meetings were more orderly." However, despite Jay's monthlong turn as chair, many men in the group continued to treat women members as inferior.

In response to this treatment, many lesbians formed women's gay liberation groups and developed an ideology of lesbian liberation that combined the concerns of both women's and gay liberation (D'Emilio 1983, 236). Groups such as Radicalesbians and Gay Women's Liberation held consciousness-raising groups, issued educational pamphlets, and participated in protests (Marotta 1981, 229–303). Even though it was crucial to these activists to create a lesbian-specific political space, the reality was that many lesbian radicals continued to participate in both gay liberation groups and women's liberation groups, and continued to persuade these movements to include lesbians in their vision of liberation (Jay 1999). The result of much hard work and conflict was a distinctly lesbian feminist ideology that exerted influences on both gay politics and feminist politics for years to come (Freedman 2002).

The gay liberation era marked a major expansion in lesbian and gay mobilization. By every measure, the movement grew dramatically. The number of homophile organizations in the United States in 1969 was fifty. By 1973 the number of activist organizations (homophile, gay liberation, and lesbian feminist) was more than eight hundred (D'Emilio 1983, 238). Membership in activist groups also swelled. Participation in the annual parade/protest march in New York City commemorating the Stonewall rebellion began at somewhere between five and ten thousand in 1970, which was a very large gay protest for the time. However, by the second half of the 1970s, these events were being held in dozens of cities across the country, with total participation exceeding five hundred thousand (D'Emilio 1983, 237–38). This increase in movement size had an even greater impact on mainstream culture, however, as the public nature of various protests brought homosexual activism into the public eye for the first time.

Gay Liberation—A New Kind of Activism

The organizations that formed in the gay liberation era emerged from several networks that prior to 1969 had overlapped only loosely. These include the homophile movement, the growing gay subcultures in urban enclaves, the civil rights movement, the women's movement, and the New Left. The homophile movement had established a history of activism on gay and lesbian issues and contributed to the gay liberation movement's tactical and rhetorical repertoire. There was also some overlap in memberships of homophile and gay liberation organizations, as several activists had been working within homophile organizations to focus more on protest and advocacy than on the social and emotional support of members, and the gay liberation movement appealed to many of these activists. However, the gay liberation movement departed sharply from its homophile roots in terms of ideology and collective identity, tactics, and grievances. These aspects of gay liberation can be traced to several other movements, especially the women's liberation movement, the civil rights movement, and the New Left.

The collective identity of gay liberationists situated them as one of many oppressed peoples fighting a corrupt social and political system. Gay liberation organizations shared not only ideologies and identities of the New Left, but also personnel. Many gay liberation activists had worked in New Left organizations. The gay liberation movement was also closely entangled with the women's liberation movement. Members of women's liberation organizations often also participated in gay liberation organizations, though many report that they felt marginalized by each of these movements (Jay 1999). Although personal interactions between men and women in gay liberation groups were often conflict laden, the ideology of gay liberation owed much to feminist ideology, which elaborated the connection between personal identity and political activism. And the rights-based claims of all of these movements, as well as strategies to use protest to guide legislative processes, can be traced to the framework put into place by the civil rights movement. The social networks of urban gay subcultures provided the infrastructure for gay men and lesbians to communicate with each other about organizations, protests, and social events. The lesbian and gay bars, bathhouses, and friendship networks provided the critical informational links necessary to support an emergent movement. Handwritten flyers, mimeographed announcements, and word of mouth were the primary tools of mobilization, and without the loose social networks of urban gay enclaves, the movement might never have taken hold.

The tactics of the gay liberation activists were both confrontational and creative. These activists borrowed heavily from the civil rights movement's tactical repertoire of nonviolent resistance but often added a campy gay style. For example, gay liberation activists targeted the New York State Liquor Authority regulation that prohibited bars from selling alcohol to homosexuals. A handful of activists, with press in tow, held a "sip-in" that consisted of visiting several bars, announcing their homosexuality, and asking to be served. When they finally landed on a bar that refused to serve them (a gay bar equally interested in overturning the regulation), they filed a complaint with the City Commission on Human Rights, which challenged the state regulation and succeeded in removing it from the books (Tobin and Wicker 1972, 69).

One critical cultural impact of gay liberation was its transformation of the meaning of coming out of the closet (D'Emilio 1983; Marotta 1981). In the homophile movement, activists were very sensitive to the potential risks of coming out, which included job loss, family rejection, and public stigma. While public acknowledgment of one's homosexuality was supported—indeed, it was considered a brave act of self-sacrifice—it was common to participate in homophile activities while closeted. This understanding of the coming-out process was changed radically by gay liberation ideology, which held that coming out was both a political act of resistance and an important personal transformation. Incorporating the feminist critique that the personal is political, liberation ideology held that to reveal one's true self to the outside world is the first step in creating a world that values sexual difference (Altman 1971).

Redefining political demands in terms of personal identity and interactions influenced the ways that activists framed their claims (for discussions of social movements and framing, see Gamson 1992; Gamson and Meyer 1996; Snow, Rochford, Worden, and Benford 1986; Snow and Benford 1988; Zald 1996). These young radicals framed their oppression as a function of a sexist society, and they often targeted police and other agents of authority, rallying anger and outrage at their harassment of, and violence against, gay men and lesbians. Regardless of how angry and forceful political claims at this time were, however, many of the political goals of gay liberation groups were reformist rather than revolutionary. Elimination of sodomy laws, relief from police harassment, and equal treatment policies were among the goals for which gay and lesbian activists fought during this time. However, even these calls for political reform often held on to a cultural critique that indicted mainstream society as corrupt, oppressive, and harmful.

Transition to Liberal Lesbian and Gay Politics

At the same time that gay liberationists were waging these policy battles, they were attempting to form new, nonsexist social spaces and egalitarian relations of power within their own organizations and in the community. In efforts to develop new institutions, some organizations rented office space to establish community centers, held dances and parties, and sponsored outings. Many activists felt that to be "out and proud," that is, to embrace homosexuality positively and publicly, was an inherently radical political act that would change negative public opinions about homosexuality. The actions of these cultural reformers were undergirded by the belief that altering public sentiment was the key element of social change. Others were frustrated by the consensus-based processes required by liberation ideology and felt that policy solutions to protect gay men and lesbians from harassment and to guarantee their rights were the more important elements of social change.

Several key leaders broke off from the first gay liberation organizations to form new groups shortly after the liberation era began, around 1970. Most of the writing on these battles within the gay liberation movement focuses on the split in New York City, where the GLF was the consensus-based, radical organization, and the Gay Activists' Alliance (GAA), was formed by a band of policy-focused activists. The GAA operated with a traditional, hierarchical structure of leadership, and meetings were conducted under *Robert's Rules of Order*. While this structure allowed meetings to proceed more smoothly and decisions about protests to be made more efficiently, critics of the GAA pointed out that all of its leaders (and most of the membership) were white men and that the voices of women, transvestites, and people of color were silenced by this structure (Jay 1999). While the GLF-GAA conflicts received more attention than similar conflicts in other cities, they were certainly not unique to the New York area. Similar struggles about political coalitions, tactics, and organizational processes plagued the Daughters of Bilitis, the Mattachine Society, Radicalesbians, and many other liberation organizations.

As Elizabeth Armstrong (2002) makes clear, these gay liberation organizations were not meant to be. The rapid decline of the New Left and its liberationist agenda coincided with the growth of lesbian and gay communities, and an identity-based movement began to emerge. According to Armstrong, this reflected the lesbian and gay community's reliance on identity as a building block of community. This wing of the movement quickly outgrew its liberation counterpart. This liberal, identity-based activism mirrored the emergent institutions of the lesbian and gay community, where a "gay and . . ." model of organizations proliferated, in which organizations like Gay History Film Project and Lesbian Mother Union used identity to tie people with similar interests into lesbian and gay-specific groups. The reconciliation of coming out and making visible lesbian and gay identities on the one hand, and the political project of procuring lesbian and gay rights on the other, led to the emergence of an identity politics project as the primary form of lesbian and gay activism in the early 1970s.

By the middle of the 1970s gay men and lesbians had made progress convincing some private employers to include sexual orientation in their list of non-discrimination policies, lobbying city and county legislators to pass gay rights bills that would make it illegal to discriminate against people based on their sexual orientation, and creating cultural events such as same-sex dances and the annual gay pride marches that continue to be celebrated in cities across the country (Gay 1978; Button, Rienzo, and Wald 1997). After pressuring the psychiatric community for years, the movement succeeded in convincing the American Psychiatric Association to remove homosexuality from its diagnostic manual in 1973. (A later version of this manual included a new diagnosis for "ego-dystonic homosexuality," but this too was removed in 1987.) Other professional associations developed caucuses for their lesbian and gay members, including those of librarians, sociologists, psychologists, and modern language scholars (Adam 1995).

Urban enclaves and subcultural gay and lesbian communities continued to thrive and expand throughout the early 1970s. Gay-owned businesses began popping up in metropolitan areas, including not only bars and bathhouses, but lesbian and gay bookstores, gift shops, and community centers. At the same time, lesbian and gay communities in smaller cities and towns began to take root, often expanding from a single gay bar into a set of community institutions and social movement organizations. Lesbian and gay student groups sprouted up on college campuses across the country, and professional academics began to come out of the closet and discuss working conditions for lesbian and gay professors and graduate students, the choice of lesbian and gay research topics, and the role of academia in setting political agendas (Crew 1978). The movement developed a division of labor, which allowed for more variety of organizational "personalities" that would appeal to a greater number of participants.

Before 1977, these two young movements did not have much interaction with each other. This all changed with Anita Bryant's grassroots mobilization to claw back some of the earliest gains of the lesbian and gay movement. Nonetheless, these historical roots account for a great deal of the opposing movement dynamics that develop in the late 1970s and early 1980s. The vast project of institution building by evangelical Christians in the middle of the twentieth century created a wealth of resources that proved very useful to the emergent religious right social movement. These include not only money, media, a dense network of para-church organizations, and a large constituent base, but also a collective identity and a set of issue frames that resonated well with a larger community. The fledgling lesbian and gay movement had a much shallower pool of resources from which to draw. Socially marginalized into small urban enclaves, with few institutional supports, entrenched anti-gay attitudes by police, public officials, and the wider public, early lesbian and gay activists still managed to organize for social change.

Given the dramatic difference in the scope of resources available to each of these movements in the 1970s, it might seem that the religious right would dominate its opposing movement, undermining all of its progress and eliminating its chance to create social change. However, what happened is much more complicated. While the religious right did undo many of the policy changes of the lesbian and gay movement, as well as hinder the progress of the movement in numerous ways, by no means did it stop lesbian and gay activism from progressing. Decades later, the lesbian and gay movement is stronger than ever. Its claims are now debated in mainstream political debates, and it has a long record of social change, not the least of which is dramatically more tolerant attitudes toward homosexuality among the American people. The following chapters will examine just how the lesbian and gay movement was able to adapt to activism of the religious right, carrying on in the face of a much richer and more powerful opposing movement.

2

The Conflict Emerges in the 1970s

I don't hate the homosexuals! But as a mother, I must protect my children from their evil influence. . . . They want to recruit your children and teach them the virtues of becoming a homosexual.

—Anita Bryant

The grassroots political activism of the early 1970s was certainly not limited to lesbian and gay issues. The cycle of protest in the United States was at a historic peak during this time period, and political and cultural changes fought for by the women's movement, the civil rights and Black Power movements, the antiwar movement, and the New Left created a culture of political upheaval and a sense of imminent change that was empowering to some but unsettling to many others. In successfully mobilizing around a number of political issues, these social movements provided an excellent demonstration that grassroots activism could be an effective path to social change (Tarrow 1993; 1994). This example was followed not only by activists with liberal agendas but also by social conservatives who wanted to halt the cultural and political changes proposed by this generation of left-leaning activists. Conservatives began to form opposing movement organizations to coordinate grassroots activism in opposition to a number of social movements.

Religious conservatives were well represented in these right-wing movement organizations, and evangelical Christians were at the forefront of the anti-abortion movement, and of the anti-feminist movement that rallied to defeat the ratification of the Equal Rights Amendment, as well as the anti-gay movement. Of these three, the anti-abortion movement proved most successful at building coalitions across religious denominations. Catholic, Protestant, and Jewish organizations worked together to limit the availability of abortions. The anti-feminist movement, though surely supported by conservative women and men of various faiths, was unified behind Catholic activist Phyllis Schlafly, whose organization, the Eagle Forum, was the flagship of a conservative movement against feminism. Following shortly after was the evangelical Christian anti-gay movement, which emerged under the charismatic leadership of Anita Bryant.

Bryant was a singer and minor celebrity who appeared on national television as a spokesperson for Florida orange juice, as well as other corporate interests. She was a friend of Schlafly and an evangelical Christian. Upon learning that Dade County, Florida, where she lived, was considering a bill that protected people from discrimination based on sexual orientation, Bryant reports that her pastor and members of her church asked her to use her powers of celebrity to appeal to county legislators to vote against the bill. Bryant agreed, and when this failed, she went further, organizing the first formal anti-gay movement organization. Save Our Children, Inc., was founded in 1977, and its members gathered enough signatures to put a repeal initiative on the ballot in the next election cycle. Bryant appeared on Pat Robertson's television show, *The 700 Club,* to mobilize support for her cause. Dade County voters supported the repeal of the lesbian and gay rights bill by a wide margin (Bryant 1977, 13–34).

Inspired by this initial victory, Bryant began a campaign to mobilize a broader anti-gay movement. Bryant renamed her group Protect America's Children due to a conflict with a similarly named child-assistance agency from Connecticut, and she began a nationwide publicity campaign to save America from lesbian and gay activists, whom she claimed were predatory homosexuals bent on recruiting children into their sinful lifestyle. Bryant's organization provided start-up funds and information to other people who wanted to repeal similar gay rights bills that had been adopted by a number of cities and towns across the country. Repeal campaigns were successful in four additional cases, and met defeat once (Button, Rienzo, and Wald 1997, 69).

Another major figure in the anti-gay movement's early days was California state senator John Briggs (R–Fullerton). His 1978 California ballot initiative, Proposition 6, would have made homosexuals (as well as those who expressed support of gay rights) ineligible for employment in the state's public school system, stating explicitly that any currently employed gay and lesbian teachers, counselors, and administrators must be fired. The Briggs Initiative, as it came to be called, was clearly inspired by Bryant's activism. Its claim that the importance of children's safety justifies the denial of equal access to employment follows Bryant's approach to the topic of gay rights, and the initiative was introduced shortly after Briggs returned from a visit to Protect America's Children's headquarters "armed with Bryant's contributor list" (Bull and Gallagher 1996, 18). However, Briggs's activism was surely also responding to the state of lesbian and gay politics in California, where San Francisco Supervisor Harvey Milk had become the first openly gay elected official in the United States, and where a number of cities such as San Francisco, Berkeley, and Palo Alto had adopted anti-discrimination bills like the ones that Protect America's Children was working to repeal (Button, Rienzo, and Wald 1997, 64). The Briggs Initiative was a statement of disapproval of San Francisco's acceptance of gay men and lesbians, and sought to demonstrate that the rest of California would not follow suit. While the Briggs Initiative was not passed by the voters, its presence on the ballot had a significant impact on the lesbian and gay movement, which mobilized quickly to form a "No on 6" campaign to defeat the measure (Witt and McCorkle 1997, 114).

The Anti-Gay Movement's Impact on Lesbian and Gay Activism

The anti-gay activism of Bryant and Briggs caught the attention of the nation. Both activists made vitriolic comments about gay men that were shocking enough to make sensational news. Bryant's celebrity status added to the newsworthiness of her activism. News of Bryant's activism soon spread well beyond Dade County, especially into lesbian and gay communities across the country. Some lesbian and gay bars began to boycott Florida orange juice, which Bryant promoted. Many have suggested that the lesbian and gay community's most important response to Bryant and her collaborators was a wave of gay men and lesbians coming out of the closet, sharing their sexual identities with their families, friends, and coworkers. Of course, the data on this phenomenon is anecdotal. That said, activists like San Francisco Supervisor Harvey Milk called for lesbians and gay men to come out as a strategy to combat the demonization of gays by activists like Bryant and Briggs. Some claim that the numbers of people who participated in lesbian and gay community events increased dramatically at this time (Marcus 1992, 259). A gay columnist who wrote under the pseudonym A. Nolder Gay (1978, 50–51), for example, claims that Christian anti-gay activists reversed a trend in which the lesbian and gay movement was losing steam: "In fact, if anything, before the Anita Bryant caper, the numbers seemed to be diminishing. The 1976 Gay Pride parades both in Boston and New York were substantially down from previous years, New York Mattachine has just gone bankrupt, and signs there and elsewhere point to a dim future for several other gay organizations." Many other popular accounts of this era indicate that Anita Bryant's national media

presence caused an upsurge in mobilization for the lesbian and gay movement, as measured by membership figures, attendance at pride marches and
other events, and financial support for lesbian and gay movement organizations. Although these impressions are difficult to confirm empirically, they
are widespread. Regardless of how many people were mobilized by the Christian anti-gay movement, it is clear that lesbian and gay movement activists
saw the opposing movement as a new sort of threat, and a very serious one.

Historical records of lesbian and gay movement organizations indicate
that a number of groups saw this new opposing movement as cause to change
the way they did their work. For example, a number of lesbian and gay movement organizations restructured their leadership hierarchy and reoriented
their agenda to prioritize political action over social events. New coalitions
between groups were established, and some new organizations were founded.
Lesbian and gay movement activists documented these organizational changes
and made it clear that their actions were being made in response to the new
threats and opportunities presented by the Christian anti-gay movement.
These changes were most readily observed in the large urban areas that hosted
sizable gay populations, both because a number of lesbian and gay movement
groups coexisted in one location and because organizational memberships
were higher there than in smaller towns. In New York City, for example,
where numerous lesbian and gay movement groups had been formed, leaders from these groups came together to form a new coalition in light of the
emergence of the Christian anti-gay movement. The Coalition for Lesbian
and Gay Rights (CLGR) described itself in its founding document as "a coalition of organizations and individuals formed to fight the attack on human
rights led by Anita Bryant and the forces she represents" (CLGR New York
1977a).

In addition to these organizational responses, existing organizations were
faced with new choices about how they would make their claims. Should they
refer directly to the opposing movement, or should they ignore it? Would
their emotional response to the harsh statements of Bryant, who accused gay
men of being child molesters, come through in their political claims, or would
they maintain a calm and professional tone? To answer these questions, I
examined historical materials produced by lesbian and gay movement organizations, such as flyers, newsletters, press releases, and letters to editors,
during the period from 1971 through 1981. The documents are part of
the collections of five major lesbian and gay archives in the United States:
the Human Sexuality Collection at Cornell University in Ithaca, New York; the
Lesbian Herstory Archives in Brooklyn, New York; the Gay, Lesbian, Bisexual,
and Transgender Historical Society of Northern California in San Francisco;

the International Gay Information Center at the New York Public Library; and the National Archive of Lesbian and Gay History in New York City.

My archival search produced 128 documents in which lesbian and gay movement organizations made political claims to a public audience, as well as some internal organizational memoranda and personal papers of lesbian and gay activists. My analysis compares documents produced from 1971 to 1976, six years prior to the emergence of the Christian anti-gay movement, and 1977 to 1981, five years after its activism began. In searching through files of materials from activist organizations and personal collections of activists, I selected those flyers, newsletters, press releases, open letters, and memoranda that contained political claims. All documents advocating some form of action (in other words, making a political claim about something that should change: a gay rights bill that should be passed, police harassment that should be stopped, and so forth) were included in these data, while other sorts of internal memoranda and organizational briefs were excluded.

My analysis focuses on shifts in language, tone, and frames used by lesbian and gay activists when making their claims. (For discussions of frame analysis and social movements, see W. Gamson 1992; W. Gamson and Meyer 1996; Oliver and Johnston 2000; Snow et al. 1986; Snow and Benford 1988, 1992; Zald 1996.) As with any historical analysis, this study is limited by the particularities of the archival collections, which may not be representative of all of the documents produced during this period. However, these archival collections comprise the best collections of primary sources of organized lesbian and gay activism in the United States.

The language category of my analysis determines whether the words used to capture the claim are inclusive or exclusive. Documents that use the words "they" or "them" or that refer to an "other" to be marked as different from the authors and readers are coded as exclusive, or "us/them." Documents that make no reference to a marked other are coded as inclusive, or "we." In a very 1970s style, these documents are often explicit about "coming together" to create change, refer to readers as "brothers and sisters," and so on, making the contrast to the exclusive documents even more marked.

The tone dimension is my attempt to capture the emotional content of these documents. My binary categorization scheme is certainly a crude measure of emotional expression, but in this case it is supported by the data, which are quite dramatically bifurcated. In some of the documents, an optimistic, enthusiastic tone is evident. Such documents educate the reader about a problem and propose a simple resolution. I code these as having an "educational" tone. Other documents contain information that is intended to inspire outrage in readers. I code these documents as "angry." I did not find any documents that were neutral in tone. I attribute this to the fact that the intent of these documents was to inspire and mobilize readers.

To code the frames, I interpret the orienting concepts of the documents by extrapolating the logic of their claims in order to establish the system of meaning to which the claims refer. (See Gerhards and Rucht 1992, for an analysis of the frames used in movement-produced leaflets. They derive the frames used in claims by identifying the structure of argumentation.) In advocating a political claim, each of the documents I analyze rests on an assumption that a problem exists that needs correcting. Some documents base their appeals for change on quests for equality and/or justice. I code these into a single "justice and equality" category. I code documents as using a "fairness" frame when their appeals are based on a more general call for fairness rather than justice or equality. Other documents assume or claim that minority populations require protection from hostile aggressors. These documents are coded into a "threatened minority" category. While the language and frames overlap considerably in the data, there is a logical distinction between these two categories. It is feasible that activists could use a "we" language to call for protection for minorities, or an "us/them" language to discuss which groups are or are not enjoying equality.

The lesbian and gay movement at this time focused their activism around three main issues: (1) anti-discrimination protections in the form of gay rights bills; (2) elimination of police harassment, especially vice raids of gay bars; and (3) eliminating the practice of unfair representations of lesbians and gay men in the media. For the most part, there was a division of labor among social movement organizations that matched these issue orientations. That is, different organizations took up different issues. Of the 128 documents I analyze, those concerned with rights far outnumbered the other two issues. I found 99 documents on the issue of rights, 17 on police abuse, and 12 on media. Fifty-eight of these documents were dated before the emergence of the anti-gay movement (1971–1976), and 70 from the period after the anti-gay movement emerged (1977–1981).

Anti-Gay Movement Causes Shift in Rhetoric

The archival documents reveal a clear shift in the way that lesbian and gay activists make their claims. However, they also reveal that this was not universally the case. The particular issue addressed by the lesbian and gay movement—police harassment, media representation, or anti-discrimination legislation—made a difference as to whether activists used a different rhetorical strategy after the opposing movement or not. Neither the claims about police harassment nor about media representation change at all in terms of inclusiveness of language, emotional tone, or frame. Documents in the later years looked very much like those produced earlier. However, most of the documents collected focused on the issue of anti-discrimination in work, housing, and public accommodations. In documents addressing this issue, which Bryant's and Briggs's organizations were directly contesting, there was evidence of rhetorical shifts in terms of language, tone, and frame. The frequency with which documents used each of these rhetorical devices is presented in Figure 1. Each unit represents one archival document, coded into one of the language, tone, and frame categories. Below, I offer some examples of the rhetorical styles of these documents, grouped by the issue of concern.

Police Harassment

The tone, language, and frames of documents on the topic of police harassment were consistent in their rhetorical strategies before and after the emergence of the opposing movement. The divisions between police and harassed gay men were made clear through an "us/them" language. The emotional tone of all the documents found was clearly angry. In all of the claims surrounding police harassment, activists represented gay men in particular, and sometimes lesbians, as a threatened minority subject to attack by police. Although documents in the later time period connected Christian anti-gay activism to police harassment experienced at the local level, the tone, language, and frames of these documents did not shift for this issue. Following are a few examples pulled from flyers and other documents.

Flyers announcing protests of police harassment used an angry tone, directly named the specific source of their grievance (either the police officers themselves or the police department in general), and proposed protest actions in the form of marches or pickets. Here is an example from a 1975 flyer from Bay Area Gay Liberation (BAGL) from San Francisco:

> Mass Gay Picket and Teach in . . .
>
> Police Captain William O'Connor's policy statement of the SFPD: "The Police Department feels that homosexuals are unsuited for police work. . . . We feel that they are emotionally unstable."
>
> Once again, the police have expressed their utter contempt for the tens of thousands of gay citizens of San Francisco. It is nothing new. Just in the past year, the police have shown their anti-gay sentiment in action. Since the illegal mass arrests on Castro Street of a year ago, a wave of heinous murders and brutal beatings have been carried out against gay people. The police have systematically failed to investigate them. . . .
>
> The present policy of the S.F.P.D. is in complete defiance of city law

Police harassment

	1971–1976	1977–1981
Language		
"we"	0	0
"us/them"	12	5
Tone		
educational	0	0
angry	12	5
Frame		
fairness	0	0
justice/equality	0	0
threatened minority	12	5

Media representation

	1971–1976	1977–1981
Language		
"we"	7	5
"us/them"	0	0
Tone		
educational	7	5
angry	0	0
Frame		
fairness	7	5
justice/equality	0	0
threatened minority	0	0

Anti-discrimination claims

	1971–1976	1977–1981
Language		
"we"	35	3
"us/them"	4	57
Tone		
educational	35	7
angry	4	53
Frame		
fairness	0	0
justice/equality	34	3
threatened minority	5	57

Figure 1. Language, tone, and frame of claims. Comparison of claims during two periods of activism: claims by lesbian and gay movement organizations before opposing movement (1971–1976) and after emergence of opposing movement (1977–1981). Each unit represents one archival document.

which forbids discrimination based on sexual orientation in all agencies of city government and in businesses contracting with the city. (BAGL 1975)

In this example, BAGL was protesting a policy statement of the police department. They did this by connecting the statement to both the police action in arresting gays and to the police inaction in investigating gay-bashing incidents. Their use of emphatic phrases such as "utter contempt," "heinous murder," and "complete defiance" drove the point home that they were angry over this issue. Other organizations also produced angry documents in which gay men were portrayed as innocent victims of malicious police. For example, the following flyer announced a GAA protest of the police violence at an earlier protest event:

> On Sunday, April 15, six gay men were brutally beaten at the Hilton Hotel. . . . The Hilton incident is only the most publicized of hundreds of vicious homophobic attempts to deny gays their civil rights. WE WILL STOP THESE OUTRAGES NOW! WE WILL JAIL OUR ATTACKERS! (GAA 1974)

This angry tone and "us/them" language remained consistent throughout both the earlier and later period for issues of police harassment of gays and their lack of concern with anti-gay violence. The following excerpt is from a flyer produced in 1979 by New York's CLGR that draws connections between police brutality and anti-gay activism:

> We Demand Justice! . . . In San Francisco last night a dozen riot police broke into a gay bar shouting, "Bonzai!" *[sic]* and indiscriminately swinging riot sticks at patrons hiding under tables. The cops yelled, "Get out you goddamned queers," and "Motherfucking faggots, sick cocksuckers!" . . . We must not forget the repeal of gay rights laws by referendum in Miami, Wichita, Eugene and St. Paul. . . . The attacks on us throughout the country are escalating at an alarming rate. . . . On October 14, 1979 all of us from New York, San Francisco, Los Angeles, Chicago—everywhere—will march on Washington, DC for lesbian and gay rights. . . . We must unite to stop them! (CLGR New York 1979)

The tone of this flyer was clearly angry; the inclusion of the police officers' inappropriate comments during the bar raid was an attempt to inspire the reader to be offended and enraged, consistent with the use of anger before the opposing movement emerged. There is urgency in the claim that attacks against gays were increasing "at an alarming rate." In this later flyer, the police brutality issue was juxtaposed against the activism of the Christian anti-gay movement, and the proposed response was to join the fight for gay rights legislation via the national March on Washington. There was very little to find in terms of a shift in rhetoric, in tone, or in the target of the police harassment. However, the Christian anti-gay movement was included in the text as an additional source of attack, equated with the police brutality, and fighting to end police abuse was presented as the appropriate solution for both of these problems.

Gay and Lesbian Representation in Media

Although the rhetorical strategies of activists' approach to gay and lesbian representation in the media were very different from those in the police harassment documents, I find a similar consistency in rhetoric over time. Documents on activism regarding media representation used an inclusive "we" language even when calling for collective action, and they consistently utilized an educational and upbeat tone. These calls to action tended to ask readers to contact local television or radio stations, and suggested a polite and friendly form of protest. Documents used a fairness frame to discuss media representation, decrying the disparity between media representations of lesbians and gay men as unhealthy, unhappy, criminal, or mentally ill and the reality of the lesbian and gay population as normal, healthy, and diverse. This tenor is present in all of the documents collected that focus on media representations throughout this time period.

Below is an excerpt from a 1975 newsletter produced by National Gay Task Force (NGTF) that announced the result of a protest against NBC for airing representations of lesbian girls as reform-school rapists in the made-for-TV movie, *Born Innocent:*

> The Gay Media Alert Network is alive—and kicking. Upon learning in advance that the lesbian television film *Born Innocent* was to be rebroadcast on October 25, NGTF sent out letters to participating GMAN organizations around the country notifying them of the re-run and suggesting ways to pressure and protest. NBC affiliates were the target of numerous sit-ins and protests. Happily, eight local stations canceled the program . . . and four sponsors withdrew. (NGTF 1975)

While the conclusion that eight cancellations was a happy result of a nationwide protest may be questionable, it is clear that the tone of this blurb was informative and positive, as opposed to the angry tone of the police harassment protests above. The target of the protest was clearly identified, as was the protest method. The message focused more on the protest work than on the source of the grievance, leaving the decision-making process by NBC in the background rather than vilifying network executives. This conveyed the

message that positive social change was happening, whereas the police brutality flyers pointed to ongoing oppression and a lack of progress. The emergence of the Christian anti-gay movement had no impact on the tone or
language of these documents, as this upbeat sentiment is also found in all of
the documents created in the anti-gay movement time period. The following press release, which was produced in 1977, incorporated news of the
opposing movement; however, the flyer's tone was still educational and the
language used was inclusive, as evidenced by its repeated usage of "we":

> We have examined the reasons for the defeat for human rights in Dade
> County, Florida, and have reached the following conclusion: the majority
> of voters did not understand the discrimination gay people actually expe-
> rience, . . . [and] their votes were based on emotional attitudes toward
> lesbians and gay men and their views on the status of homosexuality in
> society. . . . To this end, we announce our immediate plans to embark on
> a nationwide education project, the "We *Are* Your Children" Campaign
> for Human Rights. We will show the American public who we really are,
> and that we are not afraid of the truth. (NGTF 1977a)

Like the earlier announcement, the tone of this press release is pleasant; its
purpose is to inform rather than to enrage. It is noncombative, even though
this campaign to improve the image of homosexuals in the eyes of the American public was provoked by the anti-gay movement. Like the protest against
NBC, the message here was that anti-gay sentiment is simply a misunder-
standing, a matter of not having the correct information about lesbians and
gays. It used a frame of fairness and implied that the problem of anti-gay
action just required a small correction in an otherwise fair and reasonable
political world. The introduction of the opposing movement action did not
disrupt this perspective for these lesbian and gay activists, and the anti-gay
activism did not promote a major shift in rhetoric around the issue of lesbian and gay media representation. This finding is consistent throughout
the documents collected, such as in this 1977 flyer in which lesbian and gay
activists warned of the effects of Bryant's vilification of lesbians and gays in
the media:

> GAY MEDIA ALERT! Anita Bryant and her friends have embarked on a phe-
> nomenally successful media blitz, which has resulted in anti-gay editorials
> in many local newspapers and on many local radio and tv shows. It is vital
> that both the editorials and press coverage be responded to by local groups
> . . . it is vitally important to take advantage of your right to reply. (NGTF
> 1977b)

Once again, regardless of the fact that this was a warning about negative representation of gays in the media, the tone and language of the flyer was educational and upbeat, even after the emergence of the opposing movement.

Anti-discrimination Claims

For anti-discrimination claims, shifts in language, tone, and frames are evident in almost all of the documents collected. In the period before Bryant's group formed, appeals for gay rights emphasized similarities between homosexuals and heterosexuals, made appeals based on fairness and equality, and constructed parallels to the civil rights movement. Although a few documents in the period prior to the emergence of the anti-gay movement used an angry tone, for the most part, rights-based documents in the early period had a positive, educational tone, informing readers about the status of various local bills and the collective action planned to pressure legislators into passing these bills. Given this choice of tone, it is not surprising that early rights-based documents used an inclusive "we" language that pointed out the protest events, meetings, and social gatherings where a reader could go to join others in collective action, as opposed to a more divisive "us/them" language that distinguished social movement participants from an external oppressor. Claims were expressed using both a justice frame that promoted rights legislation as the way to prevent unjust discrimination, and/or an equality frame that captured anti-discrimination protection as the path to equality.

After the emergence of the opposing movement, these aspects of the lesbian and gay movement's political claims shifted dramatically. Once the opposing movement became active, documents produced by lesbian and gay movement groups invoked outrage and spoke of lesbians and gay men in the role of victim. A new "us/them" language was introduced that diverged from the earlier emphasis of similarities to other groups. Finally, documents became much more specific when referring to opponents, moving away from references to "society," "government," and "employers" to Anita Bryant and John Briggs themselves, as well as the constituencies they represented, as the locus of gay oppression. Although there were still educational components to some of the documents, these largely focused on telling readers why they should be outraged. Invoking the activism of Christian anti-gay organizations, the documents shifted away from using a more inclusive "we" language to one that distinguished between "us," a lesbian and gay audience of readers, and "them," the Christian anti-gay activists who embodied the threat to lesbian and gay rights. In this shift, the documents invoked a threatened minority frame that called for rights legislation as a protection from a hostile aggressor.

An Example: The New York City Anti-discrimination Bill

To examine the shift in rhetorical strategy in anti-discriminations claims, I present several documents from New York City–based lesbian and gay movement organizations. For the duration of the period under review, a citywide gay rights bill was repeatedly being reviewed by the city council. The bill prohibited discrimination against lesbians and gay men in the areas of housing, employment, and public accommodations. It was introduced in 1971 because of a petition drive by several lesbian and gay organizations, and it was either delayed in committee or voted down each year until a version of the bill was finally passed in 1986. During the time period covered by this research, 1971–1981, the New York City Gay Rights Bill was a constant; it was continually being considered by the council, and it consistently failed to get out of committee or to secure the necessary number of votes for passage. This bill provides an interesting window through which to view the ongoing activism of several social movement organizations before, during, and after the emergence of the Anita Bryant–led movement in Florida, a battle that had no direct impact on gay and lesbian life in New York but which had tremendous symbolic value for activists.

The organizations involved in this activism included the Gay Activists' Alliance, the Coalition for Lesbian and Gay Rights New York, Lesbian Feminist Liberation, and the National Gay Task Force. The GAA was a New York social movement organization with several hundred members. It led pickets and protests and got the word out through phone zaps and press releases with force and anger. GAA took credit for putting the first proposal for a gay rights bill, Intro 475, before the New York City Council in 1971 by pressuring council members to introduce the legislation. Their repeated calls for public support for the bill made claims around the potential for landlords or employers to discriminate against gays but did not use specific examples of anti-gay discrimination with which to ground their claims. A typical example of GAA gay rights rhetoric prior to the formation of the Christian anti-gay movement is the following 1971 flyer for a petition drive to support Intro 475:

> If you're gay you have no civil rights protection.
> JOBS? You cannot be hired. You can be fired because you are gay or because an employer thinks you are gay.
> HOUSING? You can not rent an apartment. You can not buy property. You can lose the apartment you have because you are gay or because the landlord thinks you are gay.
> PUBLIC ACCOMMODATIONS? You can be refused service at a bar, restaurant,

café, nightclub, or hotel because you are gay, or because the proprietor thinks you are gay.

"Intro 475" the Clinigan-Burden-Scholnick-Weiss bill guarantees to gay people the same civil rights that are guaranteed to other minorities. (GAA 1971)

The claims in this flyer emphasized the similarity between gay people as an oppressed group and other minority populations who experienced discrimination. The claims appealed to a sense of fairness and justice and proposed that this bill would be the one adjustment required to fix an otherwise fair and equal civil society. The message was that civil rights were guaranteed to other minority groups, and this bill was the missing link in an otherwise strong social chain. There was also an appeal for heterosexual support for the bill embedded in the repeated phrase, "because you are gay, or because [someone] thinks you are gay" (GAA 1971), which implied that homosexual rights issues extended to the heterosexual community as well.

The educational approach of the flyer implies that GAA was concerned that not all gay men and lesbians were aware that landlords and employers could lawfully discriminate against them. They must have felt that issues of discrimination were either too rare to capture the notice of the gay community or that they were hidden from general view. However, they did not supplement their educational efforts with stories of actual discrimination in these or other flyers obtained during this time period. In fact, another flyer published by the GAA called for people experiencing discrimination to come forward and tell their stories:

FIGHT ANTI-GAY EMPLOYMENT PRACTICES IN NEW YORK CITY!

If you were denied a job—if you ever lost a job—if you were ever harassed in your job because of your being gay—we need your help!!

The Fair Employment Committee of the Gay Activists Alliance needs information and testimony regarding anti-gay employers to present to the City Commission On Human Rights public hearing in late October. (GAA 1972)

Note that these data were to be used to appeal to officials in the city. In my archival search of GAA's records, I did not find any evidence that these stories were included in future political calls for action. This discursive strategy left the discriminators unnamed and left the activists to refer to only nonspecific actors, such as landlords, employers, and proprietors, as the potential source of anti-gay oppression. This strategy was different from GAA's approach to other issues, such as protests of the beatings of gay men, in which the names of specific individuals or police precincts were identified publicly.

This changed dramatically with the emergence of Save Our Children. Although Anita Bryant's successful repeal was local to the Miami area, her notoriety and the issue's salience with the press gave Christian anti-gay efforts national attention. The lesbian and gay movement in New York City could have been intimidated by the anti-gay efforts or ignored them altogether. Rather than choose either of these reactions, a number of social movement organizations decided that Bryant's activism presented an opportunity to make significant advances in lesbian and gay rights and stepped up their activism significantly, including forming the umbrella organization CLGR. This group, acting on behalf of GAA and a variety of other New York lesbian and gay activist groups, integrated opposing movement activity and rhetoric directly into its claims for passage of the gay rights bill. This 1978 flyer invokes the specter of Bryant's repeal campaign to make the case that the gay rights bill should be passed:

> For seven years, the lesbian and gay community of New York City has been fighting for passage of a bill in the City Council that would ban discrimination against us in jobs, housing, and public accommodations. . . . Things are different this time around . . . similar legislation has now been passed in some 40 cities. But the wider opponents of lesbian and gay rights are also better organized—and on a much wider scale. They have already succeeded in reversing such legislation in Miami (June 1977) and in St. Paul (April 1978). . . . These referenda represent only the beginning of a full-scale assault on the hard-won gains of lesbians and gay men. . . . They must be stopped now! (CLGR New York 1978)

There were many connections drawn between lesbian and gay movement battles in Florida, California, and New York City. These anti-gay actions, so distant in terms of the impact they would have on lesbian and gay residents of New York, were incorporated into CLGR's call for a New York City gay rights bill:

> Picket at City Hall for NYC Gay Rights Bill Intro 384
>
> Passage of Intro 384 is essential to halting the nationwide wave of anti-gay bigotry as is the defeat of Proposition 6 (the Briggs Initiative) which would mandate discrimination against lesbian and gay school employees and their supporters. If this proposition wins on Nov. 4 it would set a nationwide precedent and have a tremendous effect on the passage of our bill in NYC. (CLGR New York 1977b)

The use of the California initiative to inspire activism in support of a local New York gay rights bill was an interesting choice, exposing the lesbian and gay movement's belief that the anger that anti-gay activists like Bryant and Briggs stirred up would be a strong motivation for lesbians and gay men to join gay rights actions. CLGR claimed that passage of the New York bill would have a symbolic impact in the national fight against anti-gay activism. Of course, the New York City bill did not pass that year. The lesbian and gay activists were fighting against the inertia of a city council unmotivated to take on an unpopular gay rights bill, not the outspoken activists of the Christian anti-gay movement. Regardless, Briggs and Bryant were the banners flown to attract lesbian and gay supporters to rally for the bill.

Opposing Movements and Rhetorical Strategy

There are many practical reasons why lesbian and gay movement organizations would change from a strategy of general claims about civility and justice to one of referencing the opposing movement as a threat to the lesbian and gay community. The opposing movement grounded the claims of the lesbian and gay movement in a tangible location. Rather than referring to a potential to discriminate, the opposing movement pointed to people and rhetoric that actively attacked gay rights. Furthermore, the presence of anti-gay activism increased the sense of urgency of movement claims. Where the passage of a gay rights bill might have seemed like an inevitability at one time, pointing to Christian anti-gay activism made it clear to the lesbian and gay movement's audience that gay rights was a highly contested issue. The message was that in order to secure lasting rights, a major effort would be required.

Internal memoranda within the lesbian and gay movement indicate that this shift was not simply coincidental to the emergence of the anti-gay movement. Rather, statements within lesbian and gay activist groups indicate that this was a strategic response to new political conditions, which activists attributed to their new opponents. The NGTF issued several directives to member organizations, indicating that this organization embraced the emergence of the anti-gay movement as a public display of anti-gay sentiment, which it was trying to prove existed to the American public all along. Here is a quote from a memorandum on the topic that was distributed to lesbian and gay groups around the country:

> NGTF leaders advise that we should exploit the publicity value of Bryant's campaign against gay rights in order to explain the issues involved to the widest possible number of people. Bryant is really the perfect opponent. Her national prominence . . . insures national news coverage . . . while the feebleness of her arguments and the embarrassing backwardness of her

stance both makes her attacks easier to counteract and tends to generate "liberal" backlash in our favor. Her "Save Our Children" campaign vividly demonstrates just why gay rights laws are needed—in order to protect our people against the sort of ignorant, irrational, unjustifiable prejudice typified by Anita Bryant. (NGTF 1977c)

This reaction to Bryant's campaign is surprising, considering that for the first several months of its existence, the new opposing movement was successful in every city in which it ran a repeal campaign. The above quote is not evidence of a stunned social movement, desperately trying to salvage some good out of a sinking ship, but rather a confident movement ready to use the increased news coverage that Bryant attracted to its advantage. In terms of rhetoric, these later documents demonstrate a shift from a paradigm of sameness between heterosexuals and homosexuals, and between lesbians and gay men and other oppressed minorities, to a new "us/them" split in which homosexuals were on the defensive against them, the anti-gay activists.

The NGTF readied lesbian and gay organizations across the country to respond to every news story of the Save Our Children/Protect America's Children campaign, in order to take advantage of the new opportunity for public voice. Even when news stories did not include a statement by someone in the lesbian and gay movement in its coverage of Anita Bryant or the Briggs Initiative, their attention to the rights repeal campaign created opportunities for lesbian and gay activists to write letters to editors and demand air time for rebuttals of any anti-gay claims. Further, while the movement was tailoring its tactical strategy to opportunities created by its new opposing movement, it was also constructing a new rhetorical strategy around the threat of all the malicious Anita Bryants across the country who wanted to deny civil rights to lesbians and gay men. Movement organizations constructed Bryant's image as the epitome of ignorance and hate, the perfect example of the kind of ill will that gay men and lesbians had to deal with in their everyday lives. Bryant served as the representation of lesbian and gay oppression in the new rhetoric of the lesbian and gay movement. This was a purposeful, strategic choice by national organizations such as the NGTF, who advised lesbian and gay movement organizations to use Bryant as a stepping stone to their claims: "Ms. Bryant . . . has given us visibility and public exposure in the media to make our case. We are constantly challenged by legislators and others to document discrimination against gays; she is a magnificent example of just that!" (NGTF 1977d).

Bryant became the poster child of intolerance for the lesbian and gay movement, as did State Senator John Briggs upon the introduction of his

California initiative, Proposition 6. This flyer was created by the Bay Area Coalition against the Briggs Initiative (BACABI), which formed in response to Proposition 6:

> A collection of conservative groups—commonly called the "New Right"—are attempting to channel the anger and frustration millions of Americans are feeling about high taxes, unemployment, housing costs, the crisis within the family and the deterioration of the school system into attacks on the rights of minorities, women, public employees, the labor movement and gay people. This kind of scapegoating is similar to what took place in Nazi Germany. (BACABI 1978)

This equation of anti-gay activists with Nazis is not limited to the fight in California. In New York, former GAA president David Thorstad (1977) penned the following in a statement promoting cooperation between lesbian and gay organizations: "Our opponents are taking a page from the annals of Nazism. The Nazis first developed a final solution to the homosexuals of Germany in 1934, and then extended it to the Jews, the leftists, and other social 'undesirables.' Nazi morality was based on the same kind of Christian 'virtue' that Anita Bryant and her Nixonian cohort are using against us." These internal movement documents indicate that they were engaging with their newly formed opposing movement in a strategic way. The movement leaders who wrote these statements may or may not have been aware that they were engaging different rhetorical strategies in developing their claims, but it is clear that activists were cognizant of the potential for increased opportunities to change people's minds about homosexuality and to convince politicians to pass favorable legislation. Lesbian and gay movement activists used these new opportunities regardless of the strength of opposing movement groups locally, as the New York City case shows.

Barriers to Rhetorical Shifts

My findings indicate that the anti-gay movement provoked rhetorical shifts across geographic boundaries but not across different contested issues. Why was it that New York–based lesbian and gay movement activists were willing to invoke Anita Bryant's activism in Florida, but claims about media representation and police harassment underwent no change? Why did activists' claims about these issues remain consistent even in California, where Briggs was waging a fight against gay rights? This analysis does not provide the answer to these questions, but there may be some clues that suggest directions for further study.

One explanation might involve the organizational division of labor within the early lesbian and gay movement. In the 1970s, activist organizations tended to focus their energy on only one of these three major issues. Organizations were often created to address a single issue. For example, in San Francisco, a group of owners of local gay bars created the Tavern Guild to protest vice raids and other police harassment of bar patrons. An early national lesbian and gay organization developed a specialty wing, the Gay Media Action Network, to serve as watchdog of the mass media industry's portrayal of gay men and lesbians. Because different organizations took on different issues, the framing and language of political claims varied according to issue.

Another explanation might simply be that the issues themselves limited the rhetorical strategies available to activists. For example, the physical violence of police brutality provoked anger and outrage among lesbian and gay communities. To respond with an upbeat, educational claim for protest might seem absurd. Further, the emergence of the anti-gay movement caused lesbian and gay movement activists to use angrier tones and more exclusive language, which was already the case for claims about police harassment. But what about the pleasant, educational, inclusive claims about media representation? Why would activists not make these claims more strident, urgent, or combative? Perhaps here, too, activists may have felt that the issue must match the message. If lesbian and gay people wanted to be represented as pleasant, polite people in the media, it follows that activists would want their claims to convey this message rhetorically as well, regardless of new opportunities created by an opposing movement.

Constraints and Opportunities of Opposing Movements

These findings demonstrate that movements do have an impact on the choices and constraints of activists in an opposing social movement camp. Lesbian and gay movement actors responded to the emergence of the Christian anti-gay movement by altering their tone, language, and frames in making political claims to the state. Though the evidence presented here shows that activists were aware of the new problems that the Christian anti-gay movement presented to their cause, they also reveal that activists perceived and were willing to take advantage of new opportunities for activism. This is not to say that gay and lesbian activists did not face opposition prior to the emergence of an organized anti-gay movement. Indeed, police raids on gay bars and cruising strips were routine, and elected representatives often refused to meet with activists or acknowledge their demands (Marotta 1981). However, the opposing movement presented a new form of opposition. Anti-gay movement activists chose the social movement organizational form to reverse some of the progress made by lesbian and gay movement organizations, and on several counts, they were successful. Bryant's repeal of the Dade County gay rights ordinance, and those in a string of cities across the country, are one measure. Another measure is the explicit contest over the validity of lesbian and gay activists' "Gay is Good" motto, which the Christian anti-gay movement directly attacked, providing a cultural assault on the lesbian and gay movement as well as a political one.

As this new opposing movement set about undoing the work of the lesbian and gay movement, lesbian and gay activists saw several potential advantages that did not exist prior to that point. They had been struggling against invisibility and against political insiders who did not believe that discrimination against them was a serious matter (Endean 2006, 193–205). Many activists attempted to create a voice that would be heard by elected representatives so that unjust laws could be changed. Doing so, however, required activists to seek public exposure and to accept the accompanying risks of job loss, family rejection, and public harassment. Christian anti-gay movement activists successfully drew the debate about gay rights into the public sphere at a point where the lesbian and gay movement alone could not. Lesbian and gay movement activists who had been fighting against invisibility saw this public debate as a new opportunity for pro-gay publicity and an occasion to encourage increased mobilization.

Several lesbian and gay activists saw in the new leaders of the Christian anti-gay movement an occasion to personify the homophobic sentiment of the nation and to demonstrate their grievances in a tangible, coherent way. These shifts in strategy included building coalitions with other lesbian and gay movement organizations, increasing the number of their public appeals as press coverage of anti-gay activists afforded new opportunities for political voice, and changing the content of their appeals in response to a tangible opponent with strong symbolic value. Rhetorical strategies used to make claims moved from general calls for justice to a specific naming of the threat to lesbian and gay rights and an image of that threat embodied in Anita Bryant. The opposing movement served as evidence that intolerance toward gays was a serious social problem, lending credence to lesbian and gay activists' claims that rights ordinances were necessary. In addition to pointing fingers at the anti-gay movement, however, lesbian and gay activists making claims for anti-discrimination laws shifted from employing frames of justice and equality to frames that portrayed lesbians and gay men as a threatened minority, and these activists began using language that divided the world into "us" and "them" as opposed to demanding inclusion in civil society.

The history revealed by the archival documents discussed here demonstrates that the emergence of the Christian anti-gay movement, far from defeating the lesbian and gay movement, actually reinvigorated social movement organizations' calls to action, secured the national media attention lesbian and gay activists were unable to attract on their own, and provided the movement with a resonant and familiar symbol of oppression that they could use to capture the message of their claims. At the same time, the anti-gay movement was successfully undoing some of the legislative work that lesbian and gay activists had recently struggled to gain. The interactions between these opposing movements became integrated into the everyday work of activists and continue to be a factor to this day. This may not be entirely good news for activists on either side, but once an opposing movement stakes a claim, the particular plot of the political landscape in which social movement activists work will indeed never be the same.

By 1980, with the news of her impending divorce having tarnished her reputation among evangelical Christians and her activism experiences perhaps causing her to alter her anti-feminist views, Anita Bryant had retired (Klatch 1987, 208). Many of the local grassroots anti-gay movement organizations that she had helped to create folded soon after election day. John Briggs, whose California ballot initiative was one of the few lesbian and gay movement victories, was disappointed by the defeat, and his political career faded into obscurity. However, though the events at the end of the 1970s might have suggested the demise of the Christian anti-gay movement, it was in fact only the beginning. Soon after, the Reagan-Bush era ushered in a conservative national political context and, with Jerry Falwell spearheading the Moral Majority, the religious right as we now know it would begin to congeal. The 1980s was also the first decade of the AIDS crisis, which had a dramatic impact on lesbian and gay activism. In the next chapter, I will explore the interactions between the opposing movements in these newly conservative times.

3
Organizational Development through the 1980s

To those who insist that ministers ought not get involved in politics, I would propose two explanations: We wouldn't have to, if politicians would confine themselves to government, economics, and national defense, but today they are intruding into areas of morality and the family, attempting to legislate outside their domain.

—Tim LaHaye, Moral Majority Executive Board member

In the 1980s the lesbian and gay movement experienced a significant organizational transformation. At the start of the decade, the movement consisted of stand-alone, grassroots organizations in bigger cities and on college campuses, along with a few national organizations that were so underfunded and understaffed that their activism consisted mostly of publishing newsletters and advising local groups. Over the course of the decade, while these local activist groups in major cities and on college campuses continued to toil, several umbrella organizations and national lobbying groups were developed and expanded. Small organizations grew, new organizations were created, and others started up but could not be sustained. Unlike many earlier groups that experimented with cooperative organizational forms and rotating leadership positions, this generation of lesbian and gay movement groups was organized hierarchically. These groups set national agendas, developed tactical plans, and managed the bulk of lesbian and gay movement resources. These new, large-scale organizations could more effectively raise funds, lobby elected representatives, and direct the activism of grassroots supporters through letter-writing and telegram campaigns. By the end of the 1980s there were multiple national organizations in the United States. While some of these specialized in political lobbying, others focused on monitoring gay representations in the media, and still others concentrated on promoting national and local activism. For the most part, these corporate-style nonprofit groups were well-funded, staffed with professionals, and embedded in networks with each other and with local activists.

This might not be a surprising story. Many big corporate social movement organizations trace their roots to coffee klatches and handmade picket signs, turning after some time to a checkbook model of activism (Skocpol 2003, 174). But in the lesbian and gay movement, this organizational change was controversial. Many participants disapproved of this type of organizational development. In fact, there has been an ongoing debate about whether large-scale organizations can create the types of social changes that lesbian and gay activists want. The accusation that a particular organization is too assimilationist or caters to the mainstream has been, and to this day remains, quite common among lesbian and gay movement participants. The position of the national organizations is a difficult one. In order to make political inroads, the organization must represent a large constituency and shape its claims in a way that is palatable to large groups of lesbians and gay men, as well as to politicians and various publics. Many have noted that this leads lesbian and gay organizations to focus on middle-class lesbian and gay concerns and neglect the political demands of bisexual people, transgender people, poor lesbians and gay men, and a host of others who work in the movement. Smaller, local groups often position themselves as more authentic, more democratic, or more inclusive than large-scale, national organizations (J. Gamson 1995).

Despite this dissent, many large-scale lesbian and gay movement organizations expanded rapidly during the 1980s and continue to be active twenty years later. These big groups carry the bulk of the movement's resources and act as spokespeople for the movement in the public sphere. But it was the 1980s that witnessed the birth and rapid development of several of these large organizations and their quick rise to leadership positions within the lesbian and gay movement. In this chapter I analyze the unique political and cultural conditions of the 1980s, which not only fostered movement growth, but also pushed lesbian and gay activists toward developing formally structured, corporate organizations. I argue that the push to form these sorts of organizations, though present to some degree for all growing social movements, was even stronger in the case of the lesbian and gay movement due to two factors: (1) the public health system's lack of an appropriate response to the AIDS crisis, and (2) interactive dynamics between the lesbian and gay movement and their opposing movement.

The Changing Face of the Lesbian and Gay Movement

The 1980s was a decade of both major tragedy for the gay community and great growth for the lesbian and gay movement. As Armstrong (2002) makes clear, the development of the lesbian and gay movement cannot be well understood without sufficient attention to the larger lesbian and gay community. During the 1970s lesbian and gay communities developed very quickly, taking over new neighborhoods in some cities and turning small enclaves into vibrant communities in others. This phenomenon was mostly limited to cities, though many accounts grant too much influence to big urban centers such as New York and San Francisco and ignore the considerable number of medium-sized and smaller cities that developed community spaces around bars, bookstores, and other social institutions (see, for example, Button, Rienzo, and Wald 1997). Much of this community building occurred in the commercial sector, in businesses run by lesbian and gay people as well as in the bars and bathhouses that, though run by outsiders, provided spaces for lesbian and gay people to socialize. Commercial concerns are not often given much consideration in the study of social movements (Armstrong 2002, 113–23). However, this growth in the commercial sector supported lesbian and gay communities, including cultural venues such as drag clubs and bookstores. Similarly, commercial expansion supported the growth of lesbian and gay social movement organizations by attracting residents to lesbian and gay hubs and providing locations for the development of collective identities (Bernstein 1997).

By 1980 lesbian and gay communities were well established around a particular set of identities and ideologies (Armstrong 2002). The lesbian and gay movement, too, had undergone a change, rejecting much of its New Left ideology and developing organizations that were based around a lesbian and gay identity. The most influential organizations in the movement were entrenched in a battle for equal rights based upon an identity politics model of activism. These changes emerged in a process of dialogue both within the movement and in response to external factors, including a series of policy battles with the religious right. Battles in California and Florida informed the nation that lesbian and gay people were a threatened minority, and the anti-gay actions of activists like Anita Bryant and John Briggs inspired many gay men and lesbians to stand up for the fight and come out of the closet, increasing the size of lesbian and gay communities and mobilizing activists for the lesbian and gay movement (Marcus 1993, 69).

National Organizations

In her account of the lesbian and gay movement in San Francisco, Elizabeth Armstrong (2002, 131) marks the 1979 March on Washington as the emergence of a national lesbian and gay movement in the United States. At a reunion in New York City marking the twentieth anniversary of that momentous occasion, I listened to seasoned activists as they recalled the preparation for that march, the first nationally coordinated lesbian and gay protest in the United States, and compared it favorably to the national activism of 1999. They spoke of the hard work of the coordinating effort, which was purposely set up in a nonhierarchical way, with each local movement group coordinating its own membership. The only centralization was the vast effort of coordinating these many nodes of activism. This, the group agreed, was the way activism worked best. The activism of today, in their opinion, is too structured, too top-down (author's field notes, New York, 1999). As these activists claimed, the way that national activism is done changed dramatically between 1979 and 1999. It was over the course of the 1980s that a national lesbian and gay movement took hold, with the ascension of a few large-scale movement organizations. Each of these groups was professional, formal, and hierarchically run, with organizational forms that resembled corporations more than protest groups. Existing national organizations grew, and others were begun according to this bureaucratic, centralized organizational form. These big organizations were far from the only sort of organization in the lesbian and gay movement in the 1980s, but these groups did rise to prominence in the social movement field during this period.

The National Gay Task Force experienced great growth and continued to provide leadership for gay and lesbian movement activists nationally. In the 1970s this group worked on a shoestring budget, providing networking among activists in various lesbian and gay movement organizations across the country. For example, the National Gay Task Force was influential in the American Psychiatric Association's decision to remove its classification of homosexuality as a mental disorder. Unlike many early gay organizations, they had a history of leadership shared between men and women co-chairs, and they changed their name to National Gay and Lesbian Task Force, or NGLTF, in 1985. The NGLTF has been the lesbian and gay movement's national flagship organization, establishing itself in the field early and growing steadily over the 1980s. It provided strategic direction to local social movement organizations through its newsletter, by training local activists, and by developing resources for lesbian and gay movement organizations across the country.

The courts have been an important venue for lesbian and gay movement activism, and the Lambda Legal Defense and Education Fund is the foremost legal organization in the lesbian and gay movement. Founded in 1973, this group provides legal representation for lesbian and gay people who have experienced discrimination. In the 1980s this organization expanded its scope, challenging a federal immigration policy's ban on gay visitors and fighting sodomy statutes in a number of states (Bernstein 1997). Throughout the 1980s the group continued to take on gay and lesbian rights cases including AIDS discrimination, military discharges, child custody and inheritance challenges, and same-sex marriage cases. Lambda Legal was a consistent stronghold in the lesbian and gay movement through the 1980s.

The Gay Rights National Lobby operated in fits and starts from 1976 through 1985 as a national office from which to lobby federal politicians on lesbian and gay rights issues. In its earliest years, the group could barely raise enough money to keep its doors open (Endean 2006, 80). The Gay Rights National Lobby also worked unsuccessfully to have gay rights planks included in both the Democratic and Republican Party platforms at the national level. In the early 1980s this group was poised to be the leading advocate of gay and lesbian rights in the country. However, competition with other national gay and lesbian rights groups drove the Gay Rights National Lobby into debt, and it was absorbed by the Human Rights Campaign Fund in 1985 (Walter 1986).

The Human Rights Campaign Fund, founded in 1980, is a lobbying and education group located in Washington, D.C., that supports pro-gay candidates and lobbies congressional representatives. It is a multiple-issue group primarily concerned with anti-discrimination legislation for lesbians and gay men, reform of sodomy laws, increased funding for women's health concerns, and AIDS research and treatment. This organization, now called the Human Rights Campaign (HRC), is currently one of the largest gay and lesbian movement organizations in the United States, claiming a membership of seven hundred thousand in 2007 (see http://www.hrc.org/about_us/who_we_are .asp). HRC also sponsors National Coming Out Day, presents awards to people and organizations that advance gay and lesbian civil rights, and publishes newsletters detailing current legislation on Capitol Hill. In 1987 HRC developed a separate specialty wing, called the Field Division, to lobby Congress to prevent the enactment of national legislation adversely affecting the civil rights of gay men, lesbians, and people with AIDS. A clear response to anti-gay activism, the organization of the Field Division was similar to that of religious right groups, coordinating protest from the top down to mobilize grassroots supporters around particular pieces of legislation. The Field Division conducts "Speak Out" mail campaigns that direct messages to senators and representatives prior to legislative action on lesbian/gay, AIDS, or abortion rights issues. It also organizes a support network on state, congressional district, and local levels and maintains a congressional alert system to inform local leaders and organizations about legislative developments.

Other national organizations include the Gay and Lesbian Alliance Against Defamation, or GLAAD. GLAAD was founded in 1985 to monitor the representations of gay men and lesbians in film, television, and print media and to protest what it sees as inaccurate representations. Started in New York, GLAAD's early success protesting newspaper coverage of the AIDS epidemic led to its establishment as a national media watchdog. One of GLAAD's earliest victories was to convince the *New York Times* to use the word *gay* in the place of *homosexual* (see http://www.glaad.org/about/index .php). GLAAD has also created a program to sensitize journalists and entertainment insiders to lesbian and gay concerns.

PFLAG, Parents and Friends of Lesbians and Gays, was founded in 1981 as a network of support groups for family members of lesbian and gay people, and continues to operate in this capacity. However, PFLAG also is a large-scale, national activist organization, which claims over two hundred thousand members (see http://www.pflag.org/About_PFLAG.about.0.html). From its inception, the group distributed educational information on homosexuality to schools and churches and established itself as a source of information for the general public. PFLAG also lobbies for gay rights legislation and participates in marches and protests on a number of lesbian, gay, and AIDS-related issues. In addition to these national organizations, hundreds of local grassroots organizations emerged over the course of the 1980s. Globally, this was an era of growth in lesbian and gay organizations as well (for listings of international gay and lesbian organizations, see IGA 1985; ILGA 1988; and Hendriks, Tielman, and van der Veen 1993).

Though small, local, informally run organizations continued and new ones emerged, in the 1980s the field saw an elevation to prominence of these larger, professional, and bureaucratic organizations. Far from the small, nonhierarchical, consensus-based protest groups of the 1960s and '70s, these professionalized social movement organizations had paid staff, ran professional campaigns, and lobbied political insiders. What factors promoted this sort of organizational development, rather than others? Mayer N. Zald and Roberta Ash (1996) argue that social movement organizations do not necessarily move toward institutionalization. Rather, they respond to internal and external pressures. This chapter examines two external pressures: the AIDS/HIV crisis and the rapid expansion of the religious right.

How and Why Do Movement Organizations Change?

Some theorists argue that organizational growth occurs in a more or less uniform manner. For example, Lippitt and Schmidt (1967) claim that at some point in an organization's growth pattern, management must shift away from personal leadership to a more formal system. Others argue that the age or size of an organization determines the amount of transformation that will occur (see Barnett and Carroll 1995 for a review of this literature). Other organizational theory, however, looks to external factors to explain why and how organizations change. Much of this literature focuses understandably on the market, a primary focus of profit-seeking organizations. For nonprofit organizations such as social movement groups, however, the market is much less important to decision making. This organizational literature has been somewhat removed from the discussion of social movements, where an indirect relationship with the market changes both the internal and the external factors that are likely to promote or hinder organizational change. In the world of social movements, political contexts are more important than market considerations. Elisabeth S. Clemens (1996) argues that organizational form is shaped by competition among movement organizations and between movements and political institutions.

However, organizational theory has considered a host of other institutional factors, such as regulatory, bureaucratic, and political changes (Halliday, Powell, and Granfors 1993; McCarthy, Britt, and Wolfson 1991). DiMaggio and Powell's (1983) classic treatise on the forces that push organizations to adopt similar forms is a key insight into understanding the dynamics that would lead a social movement organization to adopt a particular organizational form. Their theory of isomorphism, or the phenomenon of similar changes in different organizations at the same time, claims that the pressures to be like others in the field can result from either mimicry or similar responses to shared constraints. Both of these factors are relevant to social movement organizations, which both learn from the successes of their counterparts in the same and other social movements and respond to shifts in political context, as Clemens notes above.

The organizational field is different in this case, however, as it is for all social movements that have to contend with opposing movements. Meyer and Staggenborg (1996, 1649) argue that movements will tend to form organizations similar to their opposing movements to the extent that they engage in the same political venues. That is, when one side draws an opponent into a ballot initiative contest, or when they each lobby senators over a bill, they will develop similar organizational structures that meet the needs of their activism. This implies that the field of lesbian and gay movement organizations will consist of some organizations that ignore the religious right and some that engage with them directly in policy battles. The former organizations should experience the pressures that Clemens identifies, while the latter group should also experience pressures to change from their opponents

(Clemens 1996). The social movements literature claims that opposing move-ments can and do alter the political contexts of their opponents (Fetner 2001; Meyer and Staggenborg 1996). For example, opposing movements can pri-oritize one issue over another and draw their opponents into policy battles they would rather avoid. Opposing movements can shift the political ven-ues in which legislative challenges are fought. Among the many potential responses to these shifting political contexts is to change the leadership struc-ture of a given organization. Another possible response is to start a new orga-nization that is structured to take advantage of new opportunities or new demands. We see both of these organizational responses in the lesbian and gay movement over the 1980s.

The religious right changed the organizational field in which the lesbian and gay movement worked in a number of ways. By increasing the public profile of lesbian and gay political issues and by directing hefty resources to political lobbying efforts, the religious right raised the bar in terms of how much fight it would take for the lesbian and gay movement to win political concessions. In addition, the organizational field was also changed dramat-ically by the AIDS crisis, which both decimated gay men's communities and pushed them to develop new forms of organizations for AIDS fund-raising and services. Below, I briefly recount these historical events from the per-spective of the lesbian and gay movement to make the case that the newer, larger lesbian and gay movement organizations that developed over the 1980s were a reasonable, if not inevitable, response to the AIDS crisis and the growth of the religious right.

AIDS/HIV

The impact of AIDS on the lesbian and gay movement over the course of the 1980s was profound. The AIDS epidemic decimated the urban gay male population, taking the lives of numerous activists. AIDS presented new prob-lems gay men needed to address, bringing into relief the poor relationship between the gay community and both the medical establishment and the state's health apparatus. The gay community's challenge to attain the same standards of medical treatment, data collection, and research for AIDS patients as for people afflicted with other types of illnesses is connected to the activist, cultural, and community-building processes of gay men and les-bians throughout the decade.

Much of this activism was provoked by the inertia of the federal health system. As the earliest cases of AIDS began to quickly add up, the federal government, led by President Ronald Reagan, was markedly silent on the issue. No federal programs to investigate this new disease were launched. No priority was given to finding the source of the illness or to discover a cure. As the new disease AIDS killed dozens, then hundreds of people in its early years, still the federal government failed to act. Federal funding for AIDS-related treatment was remarkably stingy in the first half of the 1980s (Perrow and Guillén 1990, 50–51). At the federal level, the Reagan administration was notoriously averse to increased governmental spending, particularly for human services. This tight-fistedness even kept monies for AIDS research and care that Congress had approved from reaching their destination. For example, when a test for HIV antibodies was created, Congress approved $8.4 million to screen blood supplies; the administration, however, would not release the funds (Shilts 1987, 502). Margaret Heckler, Secretary of Health and Human Services, was told that she could spend as much of her current budget on AIDS as she wished, but she would have to take it from existing programs, as no new funds would be available (Perrow and Guillén 1990, 51).

Early funds for research on AIDS were similarly tough to come by. Even as Congress approved ever larger sums of money for AIDS research, much of it did not find its way to doctors and scientists, as public health agencies declined to request any of the allocated money. Though it was clear to many that money for research was sorely needed, the Reagan appointees in charge of the agencies maintained that they already had all the money they needed. Journalist Randy Shilts (1987, 289) documents that Centers for Disease Control (CDC) director William Foege had penned a fourteen-page internal memo listing studies that needed to be done, none of which could be funded in his current budget. These internal requests were denied and were not followed by formal, public requests. Private research foundations were overwhelmed with requests for funding, and not many would make AIDS research a priority.

Even the task of gathering data on how many cases were present was an exercise in futility. From the outset, activists who gathered their own data reported that official numbers underreported both the number of cases and fatality rates (Perrow and Guillén 1990, 71). The very definition of what counted as a case of AIDS was particularly troublesome in the first half of the decade. Having decided that the real problem was the AIDS syndrome, a collection of symptoms caused by a common, but as yet unknown cause, the CDC required health officials to log as AIDS patients only those people whose disease had progressed to a severe state. Others whose health was poor but not severe were instead diagnosed as having pre-AIDS, lesser AIDS, or AIDS-Related Complex (ARC). Such a non-AIDS classification affected the type of treatment, medications, and insurance coverage to which a patient had access (Fox 1992, 126–28). Medicaid eligibility also rested upon a diagnosis of AIDS, as opposed to ARC or other pre-AIDS diagnoses (Panem 1988, 99–100).

There was also much dispute over the role of the government in public education of AIDS risks and behaviors that transmit HIV. Even before HIV was discovered as the cause of AIDS, there was key information that could have been used to slow the spread of the disease. Officials knew as early as 1982 that the cause was a blood-borne virus infecting both men and women, straights and gays, and that it could be transmitted from pregnant women to their babies. Doctors and health officials also knew that simple measures, such as bleach and condoms, could be effectively used to reduce the chance of transmission significantly. However, no education campaign was mounted at that time. In fact, in late 1985 the White House blocked the use of CDC money for education, leaving the United States behind other Western nations in telling its citizens how to avoid contracting the virus. Even as late as 1987, 45 million health information pamphlets were printed by the federal government, but bureaucratic approval processes prevented them from ever being distributed (Perrow and Guillén 1990, 26).

Most early cases of AIDS in the United States were located in New York City, Los Angeles, and San Francisco. These city governments had quite different responses to the impending epidemic. Two cities, San Francisco and New York, make a particularly interesting contrast. New York City officials were pressed to respond to the crisis from its earliest days. Since there were more cases in New York than any other city, and since the city was in charge of public hospitals, the city was the target of requests for funds and oversight of research and treatment. New York was very slow to respond, however. In 1983, four years after the first cases were discovered there, New York City was just setting up its first office to take complaints about gay and lesbian "health concerns," though no money for treatment or research was allocated, nor is there any evidence that this office was taking any actions as a result of the complaints. Hospital beds were in short supply, and many limited the number of AIDS patients they would take in (Kramer 1994, 38). Accurate information about treatment options and about avoiding transmission was difficult to come by. Mayor Ed Koch refused repeated requests to meet with AIDS activists (Kramer 1994, 58). In New York City, where 42 percent of all AIDS cases were reported, no new money had been allocated to the city's eleven public hospitals for treatment of AIDS (Perrow and Guillén 1990, 68–78).

In 1983 New York State developed an AIDS Institute to fund local service providers, but its funds were limited and it moved very slowly in reviewing proposals and awarding grants. As late as 1985 New York City's highest ranking health official, Dr. David Senser, had denied that AIDS was an epidemic (Shilts 1987, 533). In contrast, San Francisco's response was the quickest and the most aggressive in the nation (Andriote 1999, 83–85). San

Francisco, though only suffering a fraction of the total number of cases in New York City, had allocated $4 million of city funds to AIDS-related care, including the creation of an AIDS ward in the public hospital (Shilts 1987, 311). San Francisco's gay community had already made significant inroads to the political establishment, and the city quickly organized a system that was well coordinated and responsive (Andriote 1999, 83–85).

Despite the differences in San Francisco and New York City, both cities experienced a dramatic surge in new organizations to provide services to people with AIDS/HIV. In 1982 a handful of gay men in New York City raised a few thousand dollars to found the Gay Men's Health Crisis (GMHC), a private nonprofit organization that quickly became the primary location for services to AIDS patients, providing housing, food, and social support to people with AIDS and their loved ones. Not supported by federal or state funds, GMHC in its early years raised money almost exclusively from within the gay community to provide the services it could. GMHC also became the center for distribution of research and treatment information, and it quickly became the only organization to provide education, prevention, and counseling services to gay men in New York City. By 1988 it had contracts with the New York City Department of Health to deliver education and services on behalf of the city, and it had a budget of over $7 million (Perrow and Guillén 1990, 112).

In San Francisco a handful of organizations emerged in the early 1980s. The San Francisco AIDS Foundation would grow into the largest of these, playing a role similar to the GMHC in New York. Started in 1982 by gay activist Cleve Jones, and with the financial support of a few gay doctors, the San Francisco AIDS Foundation worked cooperatively with the city to deliver services to AIDS patients. This organization was far from the only one, however. Another important group was the Shanti Project, which was founded prior to the AIDS crisis as a support organization for cancer patients but quickly changed its focus to people with AIDS. It ran initially on funds raised in the gay community and later supported by city, state, and eventually federal funds. The Shanti Project operated a hospice for AIDS patients, coordinated with local hospitals, and provided services and education through its hundreds of volunteers.

People from gay and lesbian communities formed organizations to educate the public on how to prevent the spread of AIDS, to distribute condoms for free, and to distribute bleach kits to intravenous drug users so that they could clean shared needles between uses. Other organizations delivered hot meals to homebound people with AIDS or provided beds for those who lost their housing. Hospices were set up, as were homes for loved ones to stay close to the few hospitals that provided quality care for AIDS patients. This quickly grew into an AIDS movement, with multiple programs and organizations. The National Lesbian and Gay Health Foundation took the lead in collaborating with other organizations to advocate for AIDS treatment and research. A 1989 report listed over 750 organizations across the country that provided some type of AIDS-related service, and claimed that most of these programs were volunteer-run, community-based responses to the AIDS crisis (Malinowsky and Perry 1989).

Lesbians, though not afflicted by AIDS in large numbers, were on the front lines of these new forms of service provision, advocacy, and activism. Lesbians volunteered to work in many of the organizations established in the lesbian and gay community to provide services and support to people with AIDS. This included hands-on care at hospices and food banks, as well as advocacy work, fund-raising, and protest (Patton 1990). While some accounts ignore the role of lesbians in the community response to the AIDS epidemic, others have highlighted their important contributions, along with those of bisexual and straight women (Altman 1986, 94; Macks and Ryan 1988; Patton 1990). Some argue that lesbians brought greater activist experience to the movement, and that lesbians were much more likely to have feminist backgrounds, which added to this early AIDS activism. For example, Dennis Altman (1986) claims that lesbians provided crucial analysis of the social dimensions of health policy and health care, which influenced the direction of many organizations.

Because of their role in scientific and professional communities and their relationship with state funding apparatuses, AIDS organizations were much more likely to be organized around a corporate model of large organizations (Andriote 1999, 286–87). These large, bureaucratic organizations sometimes alienated the very communities from which the organizations emerged (Shepard 1997, 234–48). However, they were highly successful fund-raisers, and they provided services much more efficiently than public health organizations. The development of the numerous AIDS-related organizations in lesbian and gay communities had an impact on the lesbian and gay movement. Primarily, it took precious resources away from other sorts of lesbian and gay activism. Elizabeth Armstrong (2002, 170) reports that in San Francisco, the number of non-AIDS lesbian and gay organizations actually decreased in the late 1980s, while the number of AIDS organizations increased dramatically. Competition for resources between lesbian and gay movement groups and AIDS groups choked out some smaller organizations. At the same time, the highly successful and efficient AIDS organizations provided a new model of organizational management, as well as leadership experiences, fund-raising apparatuses, and networking opportunities for lesbian and gay movement activists, who were likely to be involved in both AIDS and lesbian and gay movement organizations. In addition, AIDS claimed the lives of a number of key movement leaders, creating opportunities for new leaders who might not share the older activists' commitment to nonhierarchical decision making and shared leadership.

By the end of the 1980s, over ninety thousand people had died of AIDS, including large numbers of gay men (Centers for Disease Control and Prevention 2001, 30). The lesbian and gay activist communities in New York, Los Angeles, San Francisco, and elsewhere across the country had been devastated by the AIDS crisis. In dealing with this tragedy, the lesbian and gay community developed strong organizations, polished fund-raising processes, and established close networks of organizations working toward common causes. All of this arose more out of necessity and survival than out of activist ideals. But when the tide turned once again to activism, there was an infrastructure in the lesbian and gay community that had not existed before the crisis, and lesbian and gay activists used these new resources when their attention turned to lesbian and gay political issues once again. The success of the AIDS organizations provided lessons for the many activists who both worked within these AIDS organizations and who remained active in the lesbian and gay movement.

The Emergence of the Religious Right

As the necessities of the AIDS crisis created opportunities to develop new organizational forms that the lesbian and gay movement could not previously sustain, the rapid growth of the religious right through the 1980s made the adoption of new organizational forms a matter of urgency. Over the course of the 1980s the religious right developed in two waves of activism. The first, led by the Moral Majority, stirred up tremendous support among a body of conservative grassroots activists who were previously apolitical. This wave was of paramount concern to lesbian and gay movement activists because of the sheer size of the movement, in terms of both participants and financial resources. This first wave of religious right activism, however, lacked the institutional infrastructure to sustain itself over the long term. A second wave of organizations, however, learned from the mistakes of the Moral Majority, creating much stronger organizations and ensuring that conservative, evangelical political activism would endure. The growth of the religious right created incentives for the lesbian and gay movement to invest in large-scale organizations. As the religious right pushed its activism into new political venues, many lesbian and gay movement leaders felt obliged to enter those venues as well.

The early 1980s was a time of transition for conservative, evangelical Christian activism. Prior to 1980 the Christian anti-gay movement was a set of local, grassroots organizations that mobilized to oppose pro-gay city or county legislation. With Anita Bryant as the movement's figurehead, these activists succeeded in defeating pro-gay legislation on a number of fronts. In less than two years, five gay rights laws were repealed in five different states; they lost one other attempt (Bull and Gallagher 1996, 17). Anita Bryant's career as an antigay activist, though an important juncture in lesbian and gay politics, was indeed a short one. In the sort of ironic twist that has befallen a number of early conservative Christian leaders, Bryant's marriage to her manager, Bob Green, was rife with conflict. Though the rhetoric of Bryant's organization, Protect America's Families, painted traditional family life as a haven from a hostile world, Bryant and Green were not able to overcome their differences, and in 1980 they announced their divorce (Klatch 1987, 207–8). As a divorced woman with four children, Bryant lost credibility with her evangelical Christian audience, and she could no longer lead her anti-gay organization or her religious group, Anita Bryant Ministries. Rebecca Klatch reports that Bryant may also have felt some feminist pangs, noting Bryant's surprise at the way women have been treated in Christian activist politics (Klatch 1987, 208). Regardless of whether Bryant had a change of heart, she did move out of the spotlight and out of anti-gay activism. John Briggs, too, faded from view. Once a gubernatorial candidate in California, Briggs made no bigger mark on the state than his failed initiative campaign against lesbians and gay men.

As the organizations led by Bryant and Briggs dissolved, however, a new set of organizations emerged. A widespread mobilization of Christian evangelicals followed closely on the heels of this early anti-gay, as well as pro-life and anti-feminist, activism on the right. This set of conservative Christian groups would come to be known as the religious right. As I discuss in chapter 1, the Christian evangelical community from which the religious right emerged had dedicated decades to institution building, community development, and networking. These institutions and communities, and the networks in which they were embedded, formed the strong foundation of the religious right. Thus, there is a wide variety of organizations, formal and informal, that might be affiliated with the religious right. Regardless, the field is dominated by large-scale, top-down organizations with multi-issue platforms. These few leading organizations manage vast resources, are densely networked, and follow a corporation style. At the helm of each of these organizations is a charismatic leader (Himmelstein 1983).

Christian evangelicals worked to embed their interpretation of Christian values into mainstream politics. Many conservative Christian evangelicals collaborated to influence Republican Party politics on a wide array of social issues, developing over the 1980s into what came to be called the religious right. Their platform included stances against feminism, abortion, divorce, lesbian and gay rights, and sex education in public schools, and for prayer in school and tax incentives for married couples. Conservative evangelical Christians, who felt that they were unrepresented outsiders of the political system, saw a new opportunity for political participation within the religious right, with a chance to make an unprecedented impact on the secular world in mobilizing their forces into a voting bloc. The new organizations that were established were large scale, well funded, and fully networked with one another, bringing conservative, evangelical Christian activism to a new level. These hierarchical organizations, with office space and paid staff, presented a polished, professional image to the public and to the elected representatives they lobbied. The organizations took up multiple issues and packaged them into one "pro-family" agenda. In this way they mobilized a large base of supporters to act on one issue at a time, targeting their efforts efficiently.

One typical example of the organizational efficiency of the religious right is the social movement organization Concerned Women for America. This group, led by Beverly LaHaye, has a national headquarters in Washington, D.C., as well as a number of state-level offices. Most of the group's members, however, interact with the organization through local "kitchen-table activism," in which small groups of women get together regularly to write letters to federal or state representatives. This particular form of organizing combines hierarchical organizational forms with traditional grassroots organizing for efficient lobbying. The issues are selected by national leaders and distributed to women who volunteer to host get-togethers where activists follow instructions about what to say and whom to write. This organizational structure features both the efficiency of centralized organizing and the political power of mass organizing, and is akin to the "astroturf" lobbying campaigns organized by corporate public relations firms (Beder 1998, 20–23).

The flagship organization of this first wave of religious right organizations was Reverend Jerry Falwell's group, the Moral Majority. In its inception, this group was really the brainchild of conservative political insiders Paul Weyrich, Ed McAteer, and Richard Viguerie. They sought to combine their influence within the Republican Party with the mass audience of Jerry Falwell's televangelist broadcasts and his extensive network of preachers across the country. Falwell became the head of this new organization, and two other early leaders in the religious right movement, James Kennedy and Tim LaHaye, were placed on the board of directors. At the same time, supporters and volunteers of the Christian anti-gay campaigns in Florida and California were mobilized into a new, multi-issue group called Christian Voice, which was the first organization to issue the "moral report cards" that later became such an integral part of the Christian Coalition's strategy.

By the end of 1980 the Moral Majority had raised $1.5 million from over four hundred thousand supporters (Diamond 1995, 174). In April 1980 a "Washington for Jesus" rally organized by televangelist Pat Robertson and Campus Crusade for Christ's Bill Bright drew two hundred thousand attendees. The split between Falwell's largely Baptist audience and Roberston's and Bright's Pentecostal and charismatic followings indicates that there was likely little overlap in these constituencies (Diamond 1989, 61). The Washington rally established 380 offices across the United States, organized by congressional district (Diamond 1995, 175). This mobilization of supporters was an important stepping-stone for demonstrating the voting power of Christian evangelicals.

The media empires that provided the backbone of the religious right were extensive. Networks including National Empowerment Television, the Christian Broadcasting Network, the Trinity Broadcasting Network, PTL (Praise the Lord)—The Inspiration Network, and Family Christian Broadcast Network offer news, family programming, and variety shows to television audiences across the country (Berlet 1998, 249). Combined viewership of religious television broadcasts in 1980–1981 has been variously estimated from 13 million to 61 million (Diamond 1989, 35–38). Radio networks are even more extensive, with over 1,200 Christian radio stations in the United States, and listeners in the tens of millions (Apostolidis 2000, 22). These mass audiences provided funds, a voting constituency, and volunteer forces for national and local causes.

The first wave of the religious right mobilized massive resources through direct-mail appeals. However, early legislative efforts to promote their socially conservative agenda did not fare so well. For example, the omnibus Family Protection Act was introduced in Congress in 1979 and modified in 1981 ("Family Protection Act," S. 1378, 1981). This sweeping bill included provisions for allowing voluntary prayer in school, tax deductions for housewives' work, termination of compulsory coeducational school sports programs, parental consent for minors seeking medical treatment for venereal disease or pregnancy, and a ban on government funding to organizations that promote homosexuality, among others. The proposed act caused much concern by activists on the left, especially in the lesbian and gay movement and the women's movement, as it was one of the first windows into the social policy agenda of the religious right. These groups mounted a challenge to the bill, but such a far-reaching set of social policies was too radical a proposal for the Senate and the bill never came up for vote (Pelham 1981, 1916). The religious right continued its conservative activism, however, and although their anti-gay agenda was not often revealed to the wider public in the 1980s, it was an integral part of the mobilization process. Fund-raising letters and Christian television and radio frequently pointed to the threat of homosexual activists. Chip Berlet reports that anti-gay letters received greater contributions than other topics (Berlet 1998, 262). Shared anti-gay sentiment aided in solidifying a collective set of grievances and ideologies, in establishing a collective identity of constituents, and in constructing a hostile enemy against which the conservative Christian activists were to fight (Herman 1997). The Moral Majority's voter registration drives signed up both unsatisfied Christian Democrats and nonvoters to the Republican Party, successfully politicizing a religious identity.

The religious right positioned itself as a countermovement against the activism that was well underway in the women's movement, the gay and lesbian movement, and what they perceived to be a movement toward "secular humanism" in the United States (for discussions of the construction of secular humanism as both a movement and a religion, see Bruce 1995, 8–9, and Lienesch 1993, 158–72). However, after a brief period of operating in the form of grassroots organizations, the movement quickly changed to a large-scale, top-down hierarchical organizational model. This form of multi-issue activism has allowed movement leaders to table their anti-gay agenda without losing their base of supporters. In the 1980s religious right activists worked on a number of issues to elect social conservatives and to influence political insiders. At the same time, they sponsored public protests over controversial issues such as abortion. The AIDS crisis provided conservative activists with opportunities to spew fiery anti-gay rhetoric, but little was happening in terms of political gains for lesbians and gay men, and so there was little to fight against. However, the attention of religious right activists turned back to anti-gay issues by the end of the decade, when protestors took to the streets demanding an appropriate response to the AIDS epidemic.

In the first wave of the religious right, organizations mobilized supporters and funds, created politicized collective identities and demonstrated mass support for a socially conservative agenda. In the second wave, which I will discuss further in chapter 4, a new set of organizations flexed their political muscle by inserting themselves into Republican circles. Overall, they maintained national networks, supported targeted letter-writing and phone campaigns, and spoke out repeatedly against what they perceived as attacks on the traditional family. By maintaining multiple-issue goals, the organizations were able to continue to influence politics on a number of issues, mobilizing their entire body of supporters for each of several issues, rather than making people choose only those issues that were most important to them. The strategy behind developing these organizations focused on the most efficient model for fighting against activism in their opposing movements, sustaining their own growth, and incorporating their issues into the Republican platform.

The Changing Field of Lesbian and Gay Activism

The organizational field of the lesbian and gay movement changed over the course of the 1980s. A set of movement groups that was largely small, grassroots, and local became a field that was dominated by a few large-scale organizations that operated on a national level. These big groups were organized hierarchically and operated bureaucratically, like corporations. I argue that this shift was primarily due to two sets of pressures in the social movement field. On the one hand, there was pressure from within the lesbian and gay community that resulted from the AIDS crisis and the government's lack of a satisfactory public health response to this disease. On the other hand, there was external pressure from their opposing movement, as it evolved into the Moral Majority and, later, the religious right.

The lesbian and gay community's response to the AIDS crisis in large part consisted of the development of new organizations dedicated to serving patients with HIV, educating the gay community and the larger population about transmission prevention, and advocating for new research on AIDS and better treatment of people with HIV. The new organizations developed to fill the gap created by a disengaged public health system, organized efficiently, and used new practices of large-scale fund-raising not previously employed by lesbian and gay movement organizations. In addition, these organizations trained and professionalized a new generation of lesbian and gay activists to do the work of running large-scale organizations.

As HIV decimated the gay population and reorganized lesbian and gay activism, the conservative movement was also undergoing significant change. The small-scale, single-issue conservative anti-gay, anti-feminist, and anti-abortion movements evolved into large-scale, multi-issue movements such as the Moral Majority and the pro-family movement. These movements had a clear, anti-gay agenda, despite the fact that little of their activism in the first half of the 1980s directly targeted lesbian and gay issues. Nonetheless, lesbian and gay movement leaders were well aware of the anti-gay agenda of the religious right. They read their fund-raising letters to constituents, watched the anti-gay rants on televangelists' shows, and saw the close ties among

Falwell, LaHaye, and other religious right leaders with anti-gay activists like Bryant and Briggs. It was clear to lesbian and gay movement activists that this new religious right represented an enormous threat to lesbian and gay rights.

The religious right had a very efficient organizational structure. It used existing Christian evangelical media institutions, churches, and para-church groups to mobilize supporters, so its organizational field contained everything from small-town, independent churches and prayer groups to giant media conglomerates. The activist organizations that dominated the field, however, were organized formally, with hierarchical leadership structures and paid professional staff. These organizations were technically independent from each other but were linked through dense network connections (Lindsay 2008). These connections often included media outlets such as television and radio shows, print media, and even entire broadcast networks. The membership, financial, and communications resources of the religious right were on a scale that was beyond the wildest dreams of the lesbian and gay movement, embodying a threat that caused a grave concern among movement leaders.

Leaders in the lesbian and gay movement saw that the AIDS crisis had given many members of the lesbian and gay community the skills and knowledge base to run complex organizations and to finance these big organizations through large-scale fund-raising projects. They also anticipated that they would need bigger, hierarchically run organizations to fight against the religious right in the numerous political battles that were imminent. In response, some organizations grew. The National Gay Task Force, the first lesbian and gay movement group to establish a national presence, grew from a small office that sent out memoranda to local groups, into a large-scale organization (renamed the National Gay and Lesbian Task Force). Other groups were founded as well, especially to provide lobbying in Washington, D.C., where the religious right's influence was strong. In the new political context, these big, national groups rose to prominence in the lesbian and gay movement.

However, this shift in the balance of power within the lesbian and gay movement was not without controversy. Although national lesbian and gay movement organizations had the support of large numbers of gay and lesbian people, many activists leveled charges of elitism, racism, and anti-bisexuality bias at them, and much time and energy has been spent on resolving issues of internal conflict (Adam 1995; Duggan 1992; J. Gamson 1995). In justifying its strategic choices, spokespeople from the larger organizations invoked the highly structured organization of anti-gay activists in the religious right. For example, in 1985 the co-chair of the Massachusetts Gay Political Caucus, Steve Tierney, made the following statement referring to the direction of growth for the national lesbian and gay movement: "There's a renewed commitment, and there's an understanding that it has to happen on an organized and professional level, because the enemy is not some scatterbrained far-right bigot, but is well organized. If we're going to compete, then we have to compete at those levels" (Freiberg 1985, 8).

As the 1980s redrew the battle lines between the lesbian and gay movement and the religious right, similar organizational forms emerged. Although some lesbian and gay movement organizations remained small and local, others took on the new political challenge posed by the religious right. These latter organizations began to adopt organizational forms that paralleled those in the religious right, although they by no means matched them in terms of size or access to resources. Still, the new organizational forms facilitated fund-raising for these lesbian and gay movement groups, which in the 1980s had far more resources than ever before. With these bigger, more bureaucratic organizations, the lesbian and gay movement was able to maintain an engagement with the religious right, dispute the claims it made publicly, and keep a watchful eye on its activities.

This development in the lesbian and gay movement was not only an effort to increase efficiency in fund-raising, lobbying, and the distribution of information to constituents. It can also be seen as an acknowledgment that the structure of the opposing movement affects both the type and the amount of work that can be accomplished. Virginia Apuzzo, head of NGTF, made this clear when she complained in 1985 that her organization did not necessarily have control of which issues to tackle: "The right always picks the fight. They always pick the issue" (Freiberg 1985, 8). Each opposing movement has to strategize not only on its own set of priorities, but it often feels obliged to respond to the other. This means that at least some of the organizations in each opposing movement must be structured in a way that counters the activism of the other side.

4

Where's the Party?
Entering the Republican and Democratic Folds

The acceptance of homosexuality is the last step in the decline of Gentile civilization.

—Pat Robertson, *700 Club*

The 1980s saw a major transformation within the religious right. The Moral Majority, led by Reverend Jerry Falwell, expanded dramatically and swiftly, mobilizing hundreds of thousands, perhaps millions, of followers (Moen 1995, 126). Just as quickly, however, this organization and others of its brief generation declined and then collapsed. By 1986 the Moral Majority no longer existed. In its place emerged a much stronger organization, Pat Robertson's Christian Coalition, as well as a host of social movement groups that identify themselves as pro-family organizations. This second generation of religious right organizations was much more politically sophisticated than its predecessors, appealed to a broader base of supporters, and had even more resources at its disposal than had the Moral Majority and its peers. While the first wave of the religious right tried to influence policy decisions by applying grassroots pressure to elected officials, the second wave was characterized by a different tactic: taking over the GOP. From the perspective of lesbian and gay movement activists, the result was a renewed opposing movement, with new organizational forms and an expanded tactical repertoire.

The young organizations in the second wave of the religious right spent the second half of the 1980s making inroads to the Republican Party. State by state, Republican Party platforms were transformed to include socially conservative positions, including anti-gay claims (Bull and Gallagher 1996,

79–82). Religious right organizations, especially Pat Robertson's Freedom Council, mobilized to take over leadership positions in the GOP, a move that would bring about a political realignment that has long outlasted Robertson's own failed bid for the Republican presidential nomination in 1988. With its political maneuvering, the religious right managed to successfully integrate its agenda into party politics at the national, state, and local levels. The takeover of the Republican Party was a major cause for celebration among conservative, evangelical Christians. Never before had evangelical Christians had such a stronghold on electoral politics as in the late 1980s, the era of the New Christian Right.

This integration of activism and political party had a strong impact on the lesbian and gay movement, which found itself pressured to align with the Democratic Party in order to have a seat at the table in the political arena. This produced a tension within the movement, whose members were well aware that Democrats were not always supportive of lesbian and gay issues. While activists knew that Democrats did not always want to align with the lesbian and gay movement, however, they needed to foster some allies among elected officials at the federal, state, and local levels to attempt to defeat the legislative proposals of pro-family Republicans. Some were hopeful, for example, about presidential candidate Bill Clinton's willingness to discuss lesbian and gay issues during his campaign. His promise to use executive privilege to overturn the military's ban on homosexuals was a sea change from only a few years before when politicians considered lesbian and gay issues too sensitive to discuss publicly.

By the end of the Clinton era, however, it became clear that influencing a political party did not necessarily translate into the implementation of social policies supported by either religious right activists or lesbian and gay movement activists. While the Republican Congress did pass a number of restrictions on access to abortion, religious right activists were frustrated with the lack of progress on this and other issues. On the other side, the debacle that resulted in the "Don't Ask, Don't Tell, Don't Pursue" policy made it clear that even executive privilege was not sufficient power to circumvent the legislative process when the issue was homosexuality.

Lesbian and gay movement leaders once again took criticism from constituents who preferred to pressure the political system from an outsider position. A number of national organizations struggled with the pressures of a Congress dominated by Republicans who were increasingly beholden to the religious right on the one hand, and on the other hand by the promise of more effective mobilization strategies outside of Washington, D.C. While courting favor with the Democratic Party was not terribly effective for the lesbian and gay movement, the fear of what might be accomplished by the religious right if resources were directed elsewhere loomed large.

The Decline of the Moral Majority

The hallmark organization of the religious right, the Moral Majority brought together conservatives against abortion, lesbian and gay rights, and women's rights. Incredibly successful at both mass mobilization and fund-raising initially, the group failed only a few years after its emergence. By 1985 Falwell was taking steps to orchestrate the dissolution of the organization. Similarly, the Christian Voice, a lobbying group led by Robert Grant and Richard Zone, downsized dramatically, suspending its lobbying efforts. This decline of the signature organization of the emergent religious right did not, however, spell the end of the movement by any means. Rather, the mid-1980s was a time of revitalization for the religious right. Early organizations declined only to be replaced by a second generation of organizations that were stronger, better organized, and more enduring than the first wave.

The Moral Majority was, in a way, a victim of its own success. The primary reason for the decline of the organization was the saturation of the direct-mail fund-raising market (Wilcox 1995, 25). The success of the Moral Majority's fund-raising efforts prompted other conservative evangelical Christian organizations to issue their own direct-mail solicitations. However, there seems to be a point at which supporters, having received too many envelopes requesting donations in their mailboxes, no longer open any of them. This saturation point was reached after two or three years, causing the Moral Majority, whose budget was primarily derived from direct-mail solicitations, to run quickly and unexpectedly out of money. Other organizations, such as Concerned Women for America, which used a membership model of activism, collecting annual dues from people who sign up, proved more enduring in the long run, and this lesson was learned by other religious right leaders. Consequently, the movement organizations that emerged in the mid-1980s were more likely to have a membership constituency.

Another reason for the Moral Majority's failure was the group's inability to deliver policy successes. The group's signature piece of legislation, the omnibus Family Protection Act, was met with more resistance than organizers anticipated, and the bill died without coming up for a vote (Diamond 1995, 232). Although the Moral Majority did gain victories in restricting funds to abortion clinics, there was little hard evidence to convince evangelical Christian followers, who were already skeptical of the value of secular politics, that lobbying politicians was the best path for social change. While Jerry Falwell was supported in his foray into politics, his lack of progress in implementing conservative social policy may have reaffirmed his core constituents' distrust of the political system. Later religious right efforts to influence policy were more scaled back than the Family Protection Act, both in terms of policy scope and scale. These efforts addressed fewer issues and focused primarily on local and state politics rather than those at the federal level.

Scholars have also cited the narrowness of the Moral Majority's base of supporters in explaining its quick demise. The organization was primarily a national one, although it did make efforts to establish regional and local affiliates. These affiliate organizations, however, were mostly under the charge of Baptist Bible Fellowship preachers. These preachers were independent religious entrepreneurs who ran their own churches without the benefit of a denomination. In addition to being time consuming, the Baptist Bible Fellowship was also known for its theocratic narrowness, which made outreach to other evangelical Christian communities difficult (Wilcox 1995, 26). Some Baptist Bible preachers made a habit of distinguishing their own followers as "true Christians" and claiming that this title did not belong to others, including Pentecostals, Presbyterians, and others who might share the Moral Majority's political goals (Wilcox 1995, 26).

Finally, the activism model used by the Moral Majority relied on a groundswell of grassroots support for each legislative proposal that the group wanted to address. In addition to the difficulties of direct-mail fund-raising that this model encountered, this form of activism is bound to create constituent fatigue sooner or later. The Moral Majority banked on its ability to deliver these letters and phone calls to representatives when legislation was on the floor, and while this was quite effective for a time, it was not sufficient in the long run. The group did not have the institutional strength to endure.

Other early groups also declined in the mid-1980s. The Religious Roundtable, founded by Ed McAteer in 1979, dissolved in 1985. The National Christian Action Coalition, which was intended to be a network among various religious right organizations, providing coordination and strategic leadership, was closed down as well. The American Coalition for Traditional Values, led by Tim LaHaye, was shut down in the mid-1980s after it was revealed that much of the group's funding was from the controversial Reverend Sun Myung Moon (Lawton 1988, 46). The Christian Voice endured a similar fate, shutting down its political activities and retooling its organization. These changes in the religious right prompted some to call the movement a failure (Bruce 1995). However, this was only a moment of transition. The organizations that emerged in the mid-1980s combined to form a much stronger and more enduring social movement than the earlier formulation. Scholars such as Clyde Wilcox (1992) mark this as the moment when the religious right grew up into a professional movement and a political power-house. The key player in this second wave of religious right activism in the 1980s was Pat Robertson.

Inside the GOP

Pat Robertson's ambitious political agenda included a conservative Christian takeover of the GOP. To this end, Robertson and his followers were suc-cessful beyond anyone's imagination. Within a decade the Republican Party would be changed dramatically as a result of the political maneuvers of Robertson's Freedom Council. Old guard Republicans were pushed out of several leadership positions in state-level party organizations, replaced by reli-gious right activists. Party platforms would reflect the socially conservative stances of the religious right. And moderate Republican politicians, for exam-ple, those who supported women's right to abortions, were in many cases squeezed out of the party. The new social conservatism of the religious right competed with and sometimes replaced the fiscal conservatism of the old guard Republicans, and it competed directly with the libertarian leanings of many in the party. This takeover process started with the quiet activities of Robertson's Freedom Council and continued with the work of his Christian Coalition and other religious right groups.

In 1981 Robertson founded the Freedom Council, a nonprofit group designed to educate voters about conservative Christian issues. Robertson began the group with funds from his broadcasting corporation, the Christian Broadcasting Network (CBN), and continued to transfer millions of dollars from the CBN to the Freedom Council for the next several years (Harrell 1988, 81). When Robertson himself entered the race for the Republican presidential nomination, it became clear that the network was supporting his candidacy, which violated the restrictions on political activity of the CBN's tax-exempt status (Diamond 1998, 73). The Freedom Council, which could conduct political activity but was not allowed to support particular candi-dates, ultimately folded while under investigation by the IRS in 1986. In the meantime, although the group was required to be nonpartisan, this organi-zation became Robertson's vehicle for mobilizing grassroots support, collect-ing names and donations, and channeling conservative evangelical Christians into the Republican Party.

Robertson targeted Michigan in particular, because of that state's early election of delegates, pouring resources into the recruitment and training of volunteers. The Freedom Council then went to work recruiting delegates in key states such as Iowa and North Carolina, where presidential candidates are chosen by caucus rather than by primary elections. The caucus procedures, which require people to attend meetings at a particular time, publicly declare their support for a candidate, and sometimes stay for hours until multiple votes are taken, produce low turnouts that make the delegate selection process vulnerable to relatively small groups of dedicated supporters. In states with primaries, Robertson focused on stacking the delegate pool with his supporters. At the GOP convention, delegates were obligated to vote for the candidate chosen by the electorate in the first round of voting but could vote their own preference in subsequent rounds of voting (Oldfield 1996, 132). Although by the time of the convention, Robertson had only 120 delegates that he had won, his group claimed that 13 percent of Bush's delegates were his supporters (Diamond 1998, 75).

Robertson's corps of campaign workers also pushed their way into state party leadership positions, not by winning the hearts and minds of the old guard GOP leaders, but mostly by taking advantage of procedural technicalities and low attendance at meetings. Freedom Council volunteers accepted positions in obscure party posts, or stacked meetings and voted their members into leadership positions precinct by precinct. This struggle for power inside the GOP was met with significant resistance. For example, in South Carolina, where Robertson supporters took control over the Charleston County Republican Party, the old guard fought back with legal action. The Robertson contingent kept their power, although the state's delegates went to Bush. In Michigan, too, the party went to the courts to decide the balance of power. Numerous counties saw dual conventions, in which Robertson supporters sponsored a competing convention. At the state convention, hundreds of Robertson supporters left the hall to form a spontaneous breakaway convention, which Robertson himself addressed. Ultimately, the courts decided that the official conventions were the ones that mattered in selecting delegates (Penning 1995, 107–8).

Pat Robertson's 1988 bid for the Republican presidential nomination was a very clever marketing tool, if not a serious bid for presidential power. Robertson told his followers that he would only run if 3 million Americans signed a petition encouraging him to do so. He maintained that this would establish the will of the people. He amassed these signatures, as well as donations for his campaign in the amount of $11 million (Boston 1996, 35–36). He had also channeled over $8 million from his Christian Broadcasting Network to the Freedom Council. This petition and bankroll became the mailing list that later supported the formation of the Christian Coalition. The Freedom Council spent most of its budget mobilizing conservative evangelical Christians to become Republican Party volunteers and delegates (Boston 1996, 37–38). In 1986 the group dissolved under pressure of an IRS audit that called into question its tax-exempt status. Though the group was short-lived, it laid the foundation for the emergence of the Christian Coalition and the religious right takeover of the Republican Party in the 1980s. In the meantime, Robertson raised over $20 million for his presidential campaign and received an additional $9.7 million in federal matching funds (Oldfield 1996, 153).

Thus, the Freedom Council paved the way for the emergence of the Christian Coalition and the religious right's movement into the GOP (Moen 1995). The Robertson campaign continued on after its demise, although it never amounted to a serious challenge for Bush. It did, however, call the attention of the press to Robertson, who invited ridicule with his penchant for making unsubstantiated claims. In addition, the multiple scandals of televangelist figures, such as Jim and Tammy Bakker and Jimmy Swaggart, none of whom were closely affiliated with the religious right or its political aims, played a role in sinking Roberston's individual political ambitions. However, the sustained attention to Robertson and the religious right substantiated Robertson's claims that the mainstream press had an anti-Christian bias, and the donations and the political support from constituents remained strong (Martin 1996, 276).

At the 1988 GOP convention Robertson gave his support to George H. W. Bush. The Bush campaign hired many of Robertson's campaign staff, hoping to retain the support of the evangelical Christian community. Moreover, Bush and his socially conservative running mate, Dan Quayle, adopted much of the religious right's agenda. Although he did not capture the presidential nomination, Robertson's political activism was clearly a success in terms of the long-term goals of the religious right. Robertson used the mailing lists, the resources, and the networks mobilized for his campaign to form the Christian Coalition, a group that would successfully break down any remaining barriers between the religious right and the Republican Party.

The Rise of the Christian Coalition

Pat Robertson used the remnants of his presidential campaign apparatus to found the Christian Coalition in 1989. Now that the religious right had a significant foot in the door of the GOP, the Christian Coalition marched forward with its plan for a major realignment of the Republican Party. Ralph Reed Jr., the fresh-faced executive director of the Christian Coalition, gained notoriety as a strategic mastermind. Together, he and Robertson nurtured their network of supporters, and one year later, Reed claimed that the group had twenty-five thousand members and twelve state chapters (Diamond 1998, 76). Their goal was to mobilize a conservative Christian voting bloc to support

Republican office holders in order to pressure elected officials to support their agenda. This successful strategy allowed the Christian Coalition to maintain the appearance of an outsider group representing persecuted Christians, while holding enormous power within the political system.

Just as the key to Robertson's strategy of gaining power within the GOP was to send recruits into the lowest levels of the party apparatus, Reed's strategy of political influence was to win elections at the lowest levels of government. County boards of supervisors, small city councils, and local school boards became the venues of choice for candidates backed by the Christian Coalition. To support the political aspirations of its supporters, Christian Coalition chapters held workshops to train people on how to run for office. Low voter turnout was the key to victory in many of these elections. Reed's mantra was the "15 percent rule," which estimates that, with voter turnouts under 30 percent it only takes 15 percent of the electorate to produce a winning candidate (Diamond 1998, 79).

Another key tactic of the Christian Coalition was to advise its candidates to run in "stealth" mode, keeping their positions on controversial issues hidden until after the election. While it had been common for religious right activists to minimize the religious basis for their political positions, the stealth approach that the Christian Coalition engineered took this voter deception to new heights. Many coalition-backed candidates did not attend debates and town hall meetings at all, nor did they talk to the press or make public appearances. Instead, they campaigned only among those who were likely supporters, using the Christian Coalition's church networks. These candidates were all but invisible to everyone except those who attended evangelical churches, and their main campaign strike came the Sunday before election day, when the cars in church parking lots were tagged with voter guides on the candidates' stances on abortion, homosexuality, and school prayer (Penning 2995, 116). The stealth approach was wildly successful in the beginning. People for the American Way, a religious right watchdog group, monitored five hundred local races and estimated that 40 percent of them were won by candidates supported by the religious right (Diamond 1998, 95). However, these victories were short lived. Most of these candidates did not survive a second round of elections. With their records more public and their deception on the table, voters by and large sent the stealth candidates packing at the end of their first terms.

These small elections, largely ignored by pundits and voters alike, became the site of substantial social change for the religious right. For example, the teaching of evolution became controversial in many school districts, with some boards opting to leave it off the curriculum or combine it with claims that are consistent with a literal reading of the Bible (Scott 1997). The content of sex education became contested as well, with religious right supporters advocating an "abstinence only" approach to sex education that excluded discussion of safer sex, condoms, and birth control. School boards received further support for this approach to sex education in 1996 when the welfare reform bill (Personal Responsibility and Work Opportunity Reconciliation Act of 1996, or PRWORA) included a measure to provide a new source of federal funding to those school districts that limited their sex education programs to an abstinence-only curriculum. In addition to eliminating discussions about safer sex, these sex education programs virtually excluded discussions of sexual identity or lesbian and gay lives. As a result of these local elections, many people across the country started to feel the effect of religious right politics in their own lives (Luker 2007).

These contests over small, local political seats were especially worrisome to the lesbian and gay movement. Just after the lesbian and gay movement had become dominated by national organizations, local politics became the site of most religious right action. Because of the demographics of the lesbian and gay community, the lesbian and gay movement had the most constituent support in urban areas on the East and West Coasts, as well as a few pockets of support in college towns in the South and Midwest. The strategy of the Christian Coalition required the massive mobilization of volunteers, relied on an infrastructure of church networks, and cost millions of dollars.

The lesbian and gay movement did not have the resources to counter this strategy directly. As religious right forces sat on city councils and school boards, the many lesbian and gay people living outside big cities and liberal pockets of the United States were increasingly vulnerable to the anti-gay policy stances of the religious right.

However, even the relatively large lesbian and gay communities in major cities could not mobilize voters in numbers sufficient to defeat the religious right in local elections. Even in New York City, which is estimated to have the largest gay population in the country, local politics produced a religious right victory in their school board's controversy over the "Children of the Rainbow" curriculum (Irvine 2002). The curriculum, which advocated a multicultural approach to education and included two books on lesbian and gay people, including the now famous *Heather Has Two Mommies* (Newman 1989), became the target of a conservative campaign that stretched well beyond the conservative, evangelical supporters of the religious right to Catholic and Jewish communities. As Irvine (2002) points out, the emotions provoked by this debate were strong, and the uproar created by its opponents caused much more discussion of lesbian and gay sexuality than the curriculum itself would have committed to sexual diversity had it been adopted. In the end, the curriculum was shelved.

Although local politics was a major focus of the Christian Coalition, the group also kept its hand in a number of state and federal elections. Because its tax-exempt status prohibited the group from endorsing candidates, it relied on what it called voter education activities. Like the Christian Voice before it, the Christian Coalition produced "report cards" rating the candidates on a number of religious right issue positions, such as abortion, lesbian and gay rights, and school prayer, and then distributed these voter guides through church networks and its own activist organizations. In the 1990 U.S. Senate race the Christian Coalition distributed 750,000 voter guides in North Carolina alone in their effort to support the reelection of Jesse Helms (Diamond 1998, 77). However, its strategy was also a long-term one, as it hoped to use local elections to nurture a pool of viable, experienced religious right candidates for higher offices in future elections. In addition, this low-level work, with its massive mobilization of volunteers, secured a broader base of support for the Republican Party.

Stronger Organizations

Of course, the Christian Coalition was far from the only organization in the religious right at this time. As discussed above, the early 1980s witnessed the emergence and decline of powerful groups such as the Christian Voice and the Moral Majority. Although some declared the movement dead when these groups declined, the real story was in the shift to stronger and more durable organizations. The Christian Coalition was at the top of this list, but it also included a number of organizations that improved on the model of activism provided by the Moral Majority. Each of these groups created real membership rolls that endured beyond the outrage of the moment, encouraging people to renew annually. They distributed newsletters and alerts that gave members a sense of the group's purpose, and they fostered a collective identity and framed their positions. In addition, the most successful of these groups gave their members reasons to belong beyond simple political activity, appealing to broad segments of the conservative evangelical Christian community.

For example, among the longest standing of these groups is Concerned Women for America. Founded in 1979 by Beverly LaHaye as an anti-feminist counterorganization to the National Organization of Women, this group avoided the pitfalls of its peers by establishing a renewable membership format and organizing its memberships around regular "kitchen table" discussion groups that provided a social function for its members in addition to its activist goals (Diamond 1998, 81). The group focused on the special concerns of women in the conservative evangelical Christian community. It has grown consistently over time, and many consider it to be one of the most successful organizations in the religious right. According to People for the American Way, the annual budget for Concerned Women for America is $10 million (PFAW 2006a).

LaHaye's husband, Tim LaHaye, is also a major player in the religious right. He has founded several organizations and has worked behind the scenes in the Republican Party. He also founded the Council for National Policy in 1981. Little is known about this group, as it is very protective of members' privacy, keeping meeting locations and member roles away from the media. However, thus far the historical record shows that this group is a network of very rich and politically powerful conservatives who come together occasionally to set the agenda priorities for the right, while donating vast sums of money to religious right and other conservative causes. Jerry Falwell has said about the group, "my guess is that literally billions of dollars have been utilized through the Council for National Policy that would not otherwise have been available" (quoted in Dreyfuss 2004, 48).

LaHaye was also the founder of the American Coalition for Traditional Values, which formed in 1981 and focused primarily on voter registration and voter mobilization. The group suffered serious setbacks, however, when ties to the controversial Reverend Sun Myung Moon were made public, and the group folded in the mid-1980s. LaHaye continued to work behind the scenes in the religious right, and he is now best known for authoring the books in the *Left Behind* series, a story of premillennial dispensation, or rapture (LaHaye and Jenkins 1996; see also LaHaye 1978). The LaHayes are an excellent example of the density of networks among religious right leaders and organizations. They met each other while attending Bob Jones University, a central node in the network of the religious right. In addition to running their own organizations, the LaHayes advise political leaders and sit on boards of directors of other religious right organizations.

In 1977 Dr. James Dobson started broadcasting *Focus on the Family*, his popular Christian radio show, which airs around the globe (Moen 1995). Out of this program, Dobson has built an organization that has been on the forefront of pro-family activism ever since. The group has avoided the problems of keeping its constituents politically motivated, because its daily focus is on more mundane issues of parenting and marriage. Dobson doles out parenting advice that coheres with a literal reading of the Bible. He is particularly well known for his support of spanking as a disciplinary technique. Dobson's following has remained steady over the decades. His public statements are more measured and palatable to a broader public than his counterparts

Jerry Falwell and Pat Robertson. As such, he does not generate as much controversy. However, this organization is a powerful lobbying force in Washington, D.C., with annual revenue currently in excess of $120 million (Preslar 2006). In addition, Dobson also founded the Family Research Council, a political powerhouse of the religious right, especially in the late 1980s when it was led by Gary Bauer, who would run for the Republican presidential nomination in 2000.

The American Family Association (AFA), led by Donald Wildmon, was also influential from the early days of the religious right. From its inception in 1977, it used a membership model and in doing so avoided the pitfalls of direct-mail solicitations. The AFA has been particularly concerned with the lesbian and gay movement, claiming to its members that lesbians and gay men are taking over schools and the government. The AFA's leaders include California state affiliate director Scott Lively, who coauthored a book claiming that homosexuals were responsible for the Holocaust (Lively and Abrams 1995). Another religious right organization particularly oriented toward issues of homosexuality is the Traditional Values Coalition, a lobbying organization whose members are churches rather than individuals. Founded in California in 1980 by Reverend Louis Sheldon, this organization grew over the decade into a powerful lobbying force that fought to maintain criminal laws against sodomy, prevent schools from giving students information about AIDS and homosexuality, and deny domestic partner benefits for same-sex couples (PFAW 2006b).

The aforementioned organizations, along with numerous others, represent a large constituency of Americans concerned with social conservatism, including opposition to lesbian and gay rights. For the most part, they are close-knit and work cooperatively. In doing so, they have built a collective identity for conservative evangelical Christians and connected this identity to a particular set of political positions. By claiming to speak for the Christian stance on a variety of political issues, these groups have obscured the variation in opinions among evangelicals (for a full discussion of evangelical political opinions, see C. Smith 2002). These groups have successfully gained power within the Republican Party, bringing both a large bloc of voters and a seemingly bottomless treasure chest. According to Oldfield (1996, 99), Pat Robertson's Christian Broadcasting Network alone rivaled the Republican Party's fund-raising apparatus, raising $230 million in 1986 compared to the $298 million raised by Republicans in 1984. To put these figures in perspective, the Democrats raised $98 million in 1984. The religious right may not have been warmly welcomed into the GOP, but once they had made their way in, few argued to kick them out.

Lesbian and Gay Movement and the Democratic Party

The religious right's rise to power within the GOP pushed explicitly anti-gay stances firmly into Republican Party politics. Whereas up to this point both parties had largely ignored lesbian and gay issues, the Republicans took the first step of putting these issues in their party platforms. However, it was not at all clear that the Democratic Party was interested in countering those positions with pro-gay stances. Rather, it seemed that most Democrats wanted to continue ignoring lesbian and gay issues altogether. The increasingly salient political presence of the religious right made that difficult to do, however, and by the 1990s politicians found that they were expected to hold a position on issues that mattered to the religious right. Abortion and lesbian and gay rights were at the top of the list. Lesbian and gay movement leaders knew that the Democrats would not necessarily become fast friends to their movement. The big lobbying groups continued their work through the 1980s, finding some politicians who supported lesbian and gay rights issues as the Republicans' ownership of the anti-gay position became solidified.

From the perspective of the lesbian and gay movement, the religious right's takeover of the GOP was a major shift in the political context. Since the emergence of the Moral Majority, there had been a difference in scale between the two opposing movements. The religious right had a much larger base of potential constituents, and their media empire provided an efficient marketing tool and fund-raising apparatus. This led to operating budgets of organizations in the religious right that dwarfed those of even the largest lesbian and gay movement organizations (Vaid 1995, 339). By the end of the 1980s, however, the religious right had more than just resources. They also had the political power to introduce and vote on legislation at the federal level, as well as in many states. This political shift was a major concern for lesbian and gay movement leaders. As Urvashi Vaid, former director of the National Gay and Lesbian Task Force, writes in her book *Virtual Equality* (1995, 339): "The answer to whether we are now organized effectively pains me, because I know how hard some activists have worked to organize campaigns and the overall movement against the right. But when our efforts are evaluated against the sophistication and skill of our enemies, the gay movement must admit to a continuing failure. Our Fight the Right efforts are as weak as theirs are strong, as scattershot as theirs are coordinated, as insignificant as theirs are effective."

The lesbian and gay movement, especially as represented by the young national organizations that had expanded in response to the growth of the religious right in the Moral Majority era of the 1980s, now faced the challenges of an opposing movement that was not only a strong influence in the GOP but was fully a political insider with numerous federal and state elected officials firmly in the religious right camp. Throughout the 1980s the lesbian and gay movement found it difficult to bring Democrats on board. Although lesbian and gay movement lobbyists found some sympathetic office holders, few were willing to take the political risks involved with supporting lesbian and gay rights. Not only was it difficult to convince members of Congress to publicly identify as supporters of equal rights for lesbians and gay men, but lobbyists found it difficult to shore up votes on an issue-by-issue basis (Endean 2006, 88). However, Republican senators and representatives, who were increasingly beholden to the religious right, were well positioned to not only block any legislation supported by the lesbian and gay movement, but also to introduce new legislative threats. Former HRC director Cheryl Jacques acknowledges the uneasy relationship between the lesbian and gay movement and the Democratic Party, despite having been a Democratic politician herself, serving in the Massachusetts State Senate from 1993 to 2004: "I don't think that all Democrats are great, but I think Democratic principles are more positive and more affirming and certainly more accepting, and more encouraging for the future of equality of gay and lesbian people. . . . No surprise that organizations like HRC are going to overwhelmingly endorse and give money to Democrats. My only caveat to that is that it's not that we necessarily had a choice" (interview with author, 2006). In this new political context, the lesbian and gay movement needed support from elected officials. In the two-party system of the United States, the Democrats were their only option.

From the perspective of Democratic politicians, however, the lesbian and gay movement was not at the top of their list of supporters to court. The voting public as a whole was perceived to be hostile to these issues, and the anti-gay forces were well organized. The political rewards for such a stance were unclear at best. Gay Rights National Lobby director Steve Endean writes in his memoir that resistance to their lobbying efforts was so strong that it was a struggle to find people to sponsor gay-supportive legislation, let alone expect to garner enough votes to win. Indeed, one of the Gay Rights National Lobby's first reports was titled "Does Support for Gay Civil Rights Spell Political Suicide?" (Endean 2006, 88). Although the report made the case that it was not, in fact, damaging to politicians to support lesbian and gay rights, the report went largely ignored. Even before the shift in power within the GOP, Democrats and Republicans alike were unwilling to vote for lesbian and gay rights. Part of the reason for this was the ambivalence of the lesbian and gay community toward national-level movement efforts, discussed in the previous chapter. Unlike the Moral Majority, which successfully in-spired its grassroots to write hundreds of thousands of letters and phone calls whenever a key vote was on the floor, the lesbian and gay community did not write letters in numbers large enough to impress its representatives. Lob-byists were told time and again that lesbian and gay issues were not important to the constituents in this district or that state, and the lack of funds made it difficult for lobbying groups to educate supporters about current legisla-tion through direct-mail appeals (Endean 2006, 247–50).

In addition to the lack of an organized mobilization of individual citizens, organizational limits added to the difficulties of national lobbying groups. Fund-raising in the conservative era of the 1980s, when lesbian and gay rights legislation was unlikely to be passed, meant that organizations operated on the barest bones. Personnel were stretched thin. Employees of the lobbying groups did the work of several staffers. Rather than produce a tight-knit group, this organizational strain promoted infighting and competition for scarce resources. The large organizations continued to struggle with those parts of the lesbian and gay community that did not support their efforts to move lesbian and gay issues into mainstream politics (Rimmerman 2000a). None-theless, over the course of the 1980s, several of these organizations continued to increase their memberships, their budgets, and their access to Democratic politicians at the federal level. This hard work seemed to pay off in the early 1990s, when Bill Clinton, then competing for the Democratic presidential nomination, explicitly pledged support for lesbian and gay rights and openly campaigned for the support of the lesbian and gay community at large (D'Emilio 2002, 136–45).

Political Parties Take Sides: The 1992 National Conventions

In 1992 Democrats nominated Bill Clinton for president. Unlike any pre-ceding presidential election, each of the Democratic nominees supported lesbian and gay rights in some form, and Clinton was right in line. For those in the lesbian and gay movement who had been struggling to gain access to the political system, this represented a major step forward. Clinton not only made promises about supporting lesbian and gay issues, but he also courted the lesbian and gay community as a fund-raising base (Vaid 1995, 126–27). For the duration of the campaign, lesbians and gay men were given more access to political contenders than ever before. To many, it seemed that the Democratic Party would be a host to lesbian and gay concerns, just as the Republicans hosted the concerns of their opposing movement.

At the 1992 Democratic national convention, held in July, Clinton used the very public stage of his acceptance speech to distinguish himself from the Republican field. In that speech he claimed that gay people were among the groups that the right had used as scapegoats and distractions from the real problems of economic mismanagement in the hands of Republicans: "for too long politicians have told the most of us that are doing all right that what's really wrong with America is the rest of us—them. Them, the minorities. Them, the liberals. Them, the poor. Them, the homeless. Them, the people with disabilities. Them, the gays. We've gotten to where we've nearly them'ed ourselves to death. Them, and them, and them. But this is America. There is no them. There is only us" (Clinton 1992). This statement was understood by many in the lesbian and gay community as a forthright embrace of gay rights. No longer were lesbian and gay movement activists on the sidelines, or worse yet, outside on the picket line trying to get their issues heard. The Clinton campaign was widely viewed as a hard-fought seat at the national table.

On the Republican side, the nominee was incumbent president George H. W. Bush. President Bush did not campaign on a strongly religious right platform, focusing instead on the weaknesses of the Democratic field. Bush was more moderate on social issues than religious right activists preferred. In protest, religious right organizations and their constituents threw their support behind Pat Buchanan, who ran a strong, populist campaign that combined a religious right agenda with a criticism of Bush's economic policies. Although Buchanan was never a serious contender for the nomination, he did get 15 percent of the votes in primary elections. Although this is not a large percentage, analysts have argued that these voters were the core constituency of socially conservative voters on which the Republicans' power rested throughout the 1980s (Abramson, Aldrich, and Rohde 1994).

At the 1992 Republican National Convention the social conservatism of the religious right became a central issue. The national GOP platform had planks opposing same-sex marriage and the adoption of children by lesbian or gay couples, as well as one that claimed that fetuses were unborn citizens with inalienable rights to life (Baker 1993). The platform committee meeting, usually managed by the campaign organization of the incumbent, was controlled by Christian Coalition supporters. More than 40 percent of all delegates at the convention were evangelical Christians. The Christian Coalition claims that three hundred of the two thousand delegates were members of its organization. On the convention floor, Republicans gave prime-time speeches to a number of religious right leaders (Oldfield 1996, 204). In so doing, opposition to lesbian and gay rights became a rallying cry for convention attendees. Pat Robertson and Marilyn Quayle each spoke at the convention, decrying the social ills caused by feminists and the lesbian and gay community (Robertson 1992; Rohter 1992).

The tone of the entire convention, however, was set by Pat Buchanan, who delivered the opening address to the convention, with his famous quote (1992, 2544), "there is a religious war going on in this country for the soul of America. It is a culture war as critical to the kind of nation we shall be as the Cold War itself." This speech, more than any other, announced the central role of the religious right within the newly organized Republican Party. It contradicted those who claimed that the religious right had declined and confirmed the worst fears of lesbian and gay activists: the most difficult battles with this enormous opposing movement were yet to come. No longer were lesbians and gay men relegated to the margins of political discourse; indeed they had been placed at center stage on the American political scene. While political parties took on the issue of lesbian and gay rights, this was not necessarily to the benefit of lesbian and gay communities. Bill Clinton's moderate support of lesbian and gay rights, evidenced by his promise to overturn the military's ban on homosexuals by executive order, represented the Democrats' commitment, while the staunchly anti-gay rhetoric of the religious right came to represent the Republicans' position.

Not surprisingly, given this political climate it seemed like a major victory for the lesbian and gay movement, as well as for feminists and other progressives, when Bill Clinton was elected president. However, the Clinton presidency was anything but a panacea for the lesbian and gay movement. Just like the religious right, the lesbian and gay movement quickly found that access to political parties and elected officials does not easily translate into policy victories. At the same time, the well-meaning new president found that even the privilege of executive order is not immune from political influence. The promised lift of the military's ban on homosexuals would turn out to be one of a series of broken promises by the Clinton administration.

Party, Not Policy

Craig Rimmerman (2000a) notes that when activism consists mostly of lobbying access becomes the goal, rather than policy outcomes. Under the Clinton administration lesbian and gay movement activists gained unprecedented access to the White House, as well as various branches of the federal government. Clinton appointed lesbians and gay men to several government positions, and his administration consulted with lesbian and gay movement groups regularly. This access, however, did not translate into the policy outcomes that lesbian and gay movement leaders had hoped for. The Clinton era produced a number of broken promises and unforeseen challenges, causing many lesbian and gay activists to argue for a reinvestment in grassroots organizing (see, for example, Vaid 1995).

The disconnect between party and policy was felt in both opposing movements. Both the religious right, which was well seated in the Republican Party, and the lesbian and gay movement, whose support was much less crucial to the Democrats, saw political returns that were more symbolic than effective, and both sides found members alienated by the political process. As the movements became affiliated with their respective political parties, however, applying pressure by withdrawing support became a less viable option. As Republicans were committed to a strong anti-gay stance and Democrats to a moderately pro-gay stance, the lobbying power of each movement was neutralized in the absence of a viable third-party option.

For example, although the Reagan-Bush era was marked by conservatism, much more policy was focused on fiscal than social issues. The early part of this era, when the religious right was a strong outsider influence, was marked by the defeat of the omnibus Family Protection Act. Even after the Christian Coalition secured insider status to the religious right, however, the Bush administration was plagued by inaction on the issues that mattered most to social conservatives. By the beginning of the 1990s religious right supporters bemoaned the lack of policy success evident through all their efforts. Although restrictions on abortion were passed throughout the country, at the federal level, the *Roe v. Wade* court ruling had not been overturned. Public school–sponsored prayer was still illegal. Lesbian and gay movement groups were larger than ever before, and the emergent AIDS movement was the loudest that lesbian and gay protestors had ever been (Wilcox 1995, 24). Although groups like the Christian Coalition and Focus on the Family were having great success mobilizing constituents, in terms of policy they were much more successful in their local efforts than on the national stage. When the political tide turned and the Democrats took office, this dissatisfaction in policymaking was also felt by the lesbian and gay movement. Despite early enthusiasm for the changing political climate symbolized by the Clinton election, it quickly became clear that winning favorable policy would not be easy. This lesson was learned early in the Clinton era, with his failed attempt to lift the military's ban on homosexuals, a subject I discuss further in chapter 6.

Strategic Decisions and Opposing Movements

The dramatic growth of the religious right during the 1980s, followed by its movement into the leadership of the GOP toward the end of the decade, produced a gross imbalance of resources between these opposing movements. While the lesbian and gay movement struggled through the AIDS crisis, the religious right amassed astounding numbers of constituents. Its groups had more volunteers and more paid staff in their organizations, and their financial resources dwarfed those of lesbian and gay movement groups. In addition, the religious right had established unprecedented access to political elites, gaining not just the ear of key politicians, but also power over them in the form of a massive voting bloc and key positions in state parties and platform committees.

While some feared that this dominance by the religious right would crush the lesbian and gay movement, it had quite the opposite effect. The religious right's strong anti-gay position only increased the political discourse around homosexuality as well as the political salience of lesbian and gay rights. Because activists in the religious right had a national stage from which to present their anti-gay agenda, they invited responses from the lesbian and gay movement. Just as the growth of the religious right promoted the development of national lobbying organizations with hierarchical leadership, the escalation of their activism called upon the lesbian and gay movement to voice their concerns. Thus, public statements and press releases would be picked up for news coverage rather than ignored. The homophobic remarks of right-wingers like Pat Robertson and Senator Jesse Helms (R–North Carolina) mobilized some to join the movement and pushed Democratic politicians to abandon their practice of ignoring lesbian and gay rights issues. The integration of the religious right into the Republican Party encouraged lesbian and gay movement activists to develop working relationships with a growing number of Democratic politicians.

Nonetheless, although the religious right amplified the voice and promoted the growth of the lesbian and gay movement, these changes were accompanied by constraints as well. Greater resources meant that the religious right had much more power than the lesbian and gay movement to select the issues that would be contested in the political sphere and to determine the venues in which they would be contested. The practice of issue selection is an important, though relatively understudied, dimension of social movement activity. Choosing which issues to fight for at a given point involves estimating public support, perceiving political opportunities, and finding a balance between the preferences of constituents and the priorities of the social movement organization. When there are opposing movements, many of the issues are shared between opponents, but their preferences for which issue to introduce at a given time are likely to be very different. For example, if one side has strong public support for a piece of legislation, they would likely want to focus their activism on securing its passage, while the opposing movement would likely want to postpone it until conditions are more favorable. In an opposing movement scenario, the movement with greater resources is likely to be the one that selects the issue to fight over. This might be due to greater access to politicians willing to sponsor legislation, greater access to media to engage in public debate, or a greater ability to pressure politicians through grassroots mobilization.

In the case of the lesbian and gay movement and the religious right, the latter had greater strength in all of these areas. It is not surprising, then, that religious right organizations in the 1980s took the lead in deciding which issues would be contested, while the lesbian and gay movement groups found themselves following the right's lead, responding to religious right claims rather than setting the agenda themselves. In the conservative political context of the Reagan era, the lesbian and gay movement may have preferred to keep its activism focused on court battles and legislative proposals in more gay-friendly local contexts. However, the religious right's push into party politics virtually required the lesbian and gay movement, or at least some of its organizations, to seek out and foster support from Democratic Party insiders.

These groups made supporting Democratic candidates a movement priority, donating to numerous campaigns at a time when, for example, same-sex sexual activity was still a crime in many states, few lesbians and gay men lived in places covered by anti-discrimination laws, and thousands of gay men were dying of AIDS. Leaders of lesbian and gay movement organizations wanted to prioritize these issues, but the political pressure they could generate was no match for the opposing movement. This frustrated lesbian and gay movement leaders, who tried to balance their own organizations' priorities with the need to put out fires set by the religious right. Cheryl Jacques put it this way: "I think this is a little bit like a river, and the current is taking you in a certain direction, and while you may paddle off to the left or the right and try to change direction here and there, at the end of the day the river is taking you in that direction" (interview with author, 2006). Although leaders in any social movement may encounter impediments to setting their policy agenda, this river metaphor is particularly appropriate when two opposing movements are so different in size as the religious right and the lesbian and gay movement.

In the 1990s the religious right once again moved away from national politics, turning back to the direct democracy tactics of Anita Bryant's heyday. This return to grassroots mobilization and street protest meant that the national lesbian and gay movement organizations headquartered in Washington, D.C., had to again shift gears and consider the weaknesses of the centralized model of activism that they had embraced. In chapter 5 I discuss the return to grassroots, street-level activism in the AIDS movement, the emergence of the queer movement that resulted, in part, from a criticism of the national lesbian and gay movement, and the role of the religious right in bringing lesbian and gay rights activism to the doorsteps of the American people.

5

Taking to the Streets: Protest and Direct Democracy

Those who practice homosexuality embrace a culture of death.
—Gary Bauer, Family Research Council

As the 1980s continued, the AIDS crisis grew, and many decried the lack of governmental leadership to address the epidemic. In response, the lesbian and gay community spearheaded numerous efforts to provide services, education, and advocacy for people with HIV. As the AIDS movement and the lesbian and gay movement became higher-profile national movements over the course of the decade, a smaller, more radical faction began to coalesce within them. This began with angry AIDS activists and extended quickly to the queer movement, a band of activists strongly influenced by poststructuralist queer theory (Duggan 1992). These self-identified radicals were less interested in engaging in identity politics than in capturing the public's attention and challenging mainstream perceptions. They used guerrilla theater and media spectacle as social movement tactics, and they relied on very public protest forms. Thus, the late 1980s and early 1990s were marked by a return to street activism after almost a decade of quiet activities and institution building.

The religious right also chose the early 1990s as a time to return to the public anti-gay activism of Anita Bryant's era. Using direct democracy initiatives to propose anti-gay legislation in two states and numerous local elections, local anti-gay groups put people on the streets with picket signs and petitions, debated lesbian and gay issues on the radio, and introduced their catchphrase, "No Special Rights," to the American lexicon. In many cases, members of these two opposing movements mobilized pickets side by side to protest city- and county-level ballot initiatives. At times in these encounters tempers flared, and singing and shouting escalated to vandalism and threats, although movement leaders on each side denounced this behavior.

As these movements opposed each other in multiple venues across many policy battles, the long-term struggle over which issues to prioritize and invest resources in became more complicated. As the religious right began to shift into new venues and invest tremendous resources in mobilizing voters and gathering signatures on petitions, the lesbian and gay movement was often pulled into fights rather than pushing its own agenda. In grappling with a geographically dispersed set of attacks on lesbian and gay rights in the form of local and state ballot initiatives, inexperienced social movement organizations led disorganized campaigns to maintain lesbian and gay rights on shoestring budgets. Although it was clear that lesbian and gay rights ordinances stood a much better chance of passing in legislative bodies at the state and local levels, the limited resources of the lesbian and gay movement were often directed toward ballot initiative battles sparked by the religious right (Werum and Winders 2001).

ACT UP

The inertia and lack of leadership by the Reagan administration in addressing the AIDS crisis fostered intense anger in gay and lesbian communities, where the perception that federal officials considered gay men's lives unimportant or even disposable was widespread. Death upon death of friends and loved ones surely fueled this anger for many, as did the frustrations of suffering from or caring for loved ones with HIV. Research on HIV was slow and, according to many, underfunded (Perrow and Guillén 1990, 50–51). The process that governed access to treatment was complicated by the experimental status of almost all treatment options at that time. The U.S. Food and Drug Administration (FDA) approval process for new drugs was very slow. Hospitals showed a lack of respect for the relationships and extended families built by gay men that were not recognized as kinship bonds under the law. Similarly, the precarious legal status of gay relationships became evident as treatment decisions, funeral arrangements, and inheritances were successfully contested by legally recognized kin, even when those families of origin were estranged from the person with AIDS. A host of other legal issues that involve kinship ties, such as housing and child custody, fell upon the gay community at once, making the legal status of same-sex relationships highly salient in lesbian and gay communities (Altman 1986).

Existing AIDS organizations focused primarily on providing services to communities. As the years went on, these groups increasingly collaborated with government officials to seek funding, coordinate programs, and stream-line services. AIDS groups generally did not see themselves as social move-ment organizations. They were not equipped to deal with or channel the anger building up in lesbian and gay communities, and the leaders of these orga-nizations did not want to jeopardize their groups' reputations or their fledg-ling ties to bureaucratic agencies and funding sources. From the beginning, some members of these organizations called upon them to be advocates for AIDS patients, rather than just service providers, but these challenges were largely unsuccessful (Kramer 1983). As time went on, the conflict within these organizations boiled over, and the number of people concerned with AIDS activism, in addition to AIDS service and treatment, grew.

In 1987 the AIDS Coalition to Unleash Power (ACT UP) was formed in New York City and began a new cycle of public protest against the lack of attention to the AIDS crisis. ACT UP grabbed the attention of the press with its dramatic protests, including mock funerals and throwing of blood in public places (most, if not all, of this blood was fake, though some have claimed that actual, HIV-infected blood was also thrown). Local ACT UP groups sprouted up across the country, and protests were aimed at the het-erosexist visiting policies of many hospitals, the lack of adequate federal fund-ing for research, and the slow drug approval processes at the FDA. ACT UP and other protest organizations that formed in the late 1980s provided a re-birth of dramatic, angry protest regarding the treatment of AIDS patients in particular and the gay community in general (Gould 2002). While other marginalized populations were also afflicted with HIV and may have been treated just as badly as gay men who contracted the virus, the social under-standing of AIDS as a gay disease and the impressive response to the crisis by the gay community combined to make AIDS a gay issue, even at the end of the decade (for a discussion of the conflict in AIDS activism over this issue, see J. Gamson 1989).

The activists in ACT UP were media savvy, and their tactical choices reflected a reliance on marketing techniques, such as branding, that had for-merly been associated with the corporate world. The group's logo, the pink triangle used by Nazis to mark homosexuals in concentration camps, com-bined with its slogan, "Silence=Death," expressed symbolically the violence embedded in the inaction that characterized the government's response to the AIDS crisis, as it implicated all those who did not raise their voices in protest. This logo spread quickly on T-shirts and buttons throughout lesbian and gay communities and beyond, an elegant statement of protest and a uni-fying symbol that revealed the breadth of criticism of the government's re-sponse to the crisis and, to some extent, support for lesbian and gay people.

ACT UP mobilized large numbers of supporters very quickly, and the organization soon had loosely affiliated chapters throughout the country. They targeted multiple sites for protest, including the federal government and its agencies, particularly the FDA. They also targeted pharmaceutical manufacturers that charged exorbitant prices for early AIDS drugs and the New York Stock Exchange on Wall Street, where protestors accused big business of profiting from AIDS. ACT UP protestors staged mock funerals and die-ins. They lay down in busy intersections and blocked traffic in many cities. The guerrilla theater of ACT UP's protests caught the attention of news media, making the organization's activities, if not its political agenda, well known in a short period of time. The activists are credited with a number of victories, including pushing the government to fund research on HIV, changing the FDA's process for testing experimental drugs, and convincing drug companies to lower prices. Perhaps ACT UP's greatest accomplishment, however, was cultural: breaking the silence surrounding AIDS both within and beyond lesbian and gay communities.

Queer Nation

In 1990 a group of ACT UP activists in New York formed a new lesbian and gay group, Queer Nation. Inspired by the victories of ACT UP but wanting to expand to non-AIDS issues facing lesbian and gay communities, Queer Nation quickly became the self-proclaimed radical wing of the lesbian and gay movement. During its approximately two-year lifespan this group specialized in direct action protest around all sorts of political issues regarding sexual nonconformity. Equally critical of the government, anti-gay activists, and the now highly institutionalized portion of the lesbian and gay movement, Queer Nation stood for those who were marginalized by social norms of sexuality, including not only gay men and lesbians but also transgender people, bisexuals, and people who participate in sexual role play, partner swapping, and BDSM (bondage, domination, and sadism and masochism) (Duggan 1992).

Those involved in Queer Nation and with queer politics in general were influenced greatly by queer theory, which criticizes traditional concepts of roles and identities as too rigid and structured and points instead to the fluidity of sexuality, including the ability of individuals to adopt multiple roles simultaneously or switch quickly from one role to another (S. Epstein 1999, 60–64; Seidman 1993). From this perspective, the lesbian and gay movement's reliance on building a constituency through a shared lesbian or gay identity was defined as part of the problem to be addressed by queer activists. Activists in Queer Nation accused the identity politics of the mainstream lesbian and gay movement of excluding members of queer communities and other allies.

Further, they considered the lesbian and gay movement's reformist goals of equal rights and fair treatment to be assimilationist, pandering to the social norms that marginalize queer people (Gamson 1995).

Queer Nation also rejected the organizational structure of the national lesbian and gay movement groups. While the national organizations relied on hierarchical organizational models from the private, corporate sector, Queer Nation operated with as little organizational structure as possible. The name "Queer Nation" was really all that connected the myriad independent groups of activists, each of which organized their own groups as they saw fit. The original group in New York City chose to have only meetings run by rotating leaders rather than institute a set of roles to be performed. Instead, action groups were created when someone had a creative idea for a protest. Whoever was interested in pursuing that idea joined the action group, shared in the work, and provided a protest opportunity for the group as a whole to join. No approval from the larger group was required; rather, all actions had a priori approval, and any action group had permission to use the name Queer Nation for any protest they chose. This organizational style encouraged creativity and drama, as well as pushing the envelope of what was considered a normal or acceptable protest activity (Queer National Steve [pseudonym], interview with author, 2002).

Although Queer Nation did not have a formalized agenda, a retrospective look at its protest targets makes it clear that Queer Nationals, as some members called themselves, were less concerned with policy and legislation than with cultural targets such as social norms, media representations, queer visibility, and cultural messages about sexuality and gender. This radical identity did not so much reflect a desire to change the government as it did a desire to create a cultural revolution in which sexuality was freer, sexual norms were less constrictive, and sexual and gender boundaries were blurred. Thus, Queer Nation harkened back to the era of gay liberationist politics with its focus on the queerness of all people rather than the lesbian and gay identities of some.

To affect these changes, members relied on dramatic, theatrical protests designed to capture the attention of passers by and the news media alike. One favored protest tactic was the "kiss-in," where members of Queer Nation would kiss in same-sex pairs in a public space. Shopping malls in the suburbs, where the shock value would be the greatest, were common protest sites. During or after the kiss-in, members would hand out educational tools for their audience, such as leaflets about gay and lesbian youth, available community service supports, and so on. The Queer Shopping Network, in which participants would go to a mall or urban shopping district and make a theatrical display of their consumer activities to demonstrate that mainstream businesses were supported by queer money, was another key protest event that had its roots in the days of gay liberation. Activists in Queer Nation performed acts of civil disobedience akin to the activities of other protest groups, but the unique quality of the members of this group was their unapologetic attitude about their non-normative sexuality. As they marched in parades and pickets, they would chant, "we're here . . . we're queer . . . get used to it!"

One particularly controversial act associated with ACT UP and Queer Nation was the practice of "outing" closeted gay public officials who did not support the gay community. In Oregon, ACT UP held a protest over an anti-gay vote by State Senator Mark Hatfield, claiming he was gay (Gross 1993, 38). In Illinois, Chicago ACT UP members protested outside the home of Governor James Thompson carrying picket signs declaring he was gay, in response to his support for legislation authorizing HIV testing without patients' consent (Gross 1993, 38). In 1991 Queer Nation activist Michael Petrelis claimed that the Assistant Secretary of Defense, Pete Williams, was gay, in an attempt to expose the hypocrisy of the military, which considered homosexuals unfit for military service (Signorile 1991, 91). In 1992 Louisiana Representative Jim McCrery, a Republican who supported the religious right's platform of "family values," was outed by a former sex partner, though McCrery denied the claim (Bull 1992, 38). Those in support of outing argued that by agreeing to protect the identities of closeted people who participate in gay life, the community was playing a role in supporting the anti-gay portrayals and policies that these individuals supported in their public roles (Goldstein 1991, 98). Those against outing argued that the practice was a betrayal of confidence and an invasion of privacy (Mohr 1992, 11–48).

Although Queer Nation considered itself to be a radical movement, the biggest successes attributed to its activism were reformist, not revolutionary. For example, mainstream lesbian and gay activists who took seriously the arguments of queer activists pushed their organizations to be more inclusive of a wider set of constituents. Without fully embracing the goals of queer activists, many lesbian and gay organizations changed their organizational identities to include bisexual people and transgender people and made some strides to include bisexuality and transgender issues in their agendas. By the mid-1990s the lesbian and gay movement considered itself an "LGBT" movement (for lesbian, gay, bisexual, and transgender people), although lesbian and gay men's politics remained the highest priorities for most organizations. In addition, newer social movement groups representing bisexual, transgender, or transsexual people began to develop their own memberships and secure a foothold for activism in the political landscape over the course of the decade.

Queer Nation's primary goal of redefining social norms to be more inclusive of a wider range of sexual behaviors and identities proved more difficult to achieve, as did its ability to sustain itself as an organization. By the end of 1992 Queer Nation was all but through, with just a few activists hanging on, putting together protests that were poorly attended. However, although it was short lived, this movement had an important impact not only on the lesbian and gay movement, but also on the sphere of contested politics over legislative battles, in which it was not particularly interested. The jarring of cultural norms that the Queer Nation protestors began was picked up and amplified by organizations in the religious right who used similar theatrical protests to mobilize their constituents against the lesbian and gay movement overall.

To capture the attention of the media and the public, ACT UP and Queer Nation activists sarcastically played the role of the menacing homosexual painted by the religious right. ACT UP New York's most memorable, and infamous, protest event is a case in point. In 1989 ACT UP staged a protest in New York's St. Patrick's Cathedral, where the highest-ranking Catholic in the city, John Cardinal O'Connor, was delivering mass, and where the city's mayor, Ed Koch, was in attendance. The protestors interrupted the mass by standing up and shouting condemnations of the Catholic Church. Protestors threw condoms and chained themselves to pews. Throughout the 1980s the Catholic Church had opposed public distribution of condoms, funding of AIDS wards in city hospitals, and distribution of information about the disease, especially through sex education in public schools. ACT UP protestors had chosen this target to highlight the lack of separation of church and state regarding the AIDS crisis, and to expose the back-room dealings between the church and the city government. Dozens of protestors were arrested. This protest was widely criticized in the mainstream press, and it was controversial within the lesbian and gay movement as well. Many lesbian and gay movement groups condemned the invasion of such a sacred place. Activists and pundits alike debated for weeks the merits and offenses of this act and, in so doing, brought a broader awareness of the politics of AIDS to the public. ACT UP New York considered the event a major success on this front.

In other protests, Queer Nation and ACT UP criticized and ridiculed religious institutions in general, and the religious right movement in particular. They often did this by projecting an image of the scary menace that leaders in the religious right had painted of them. In parades and other protests Queer Nation and ACT UP protestors would mock the claims of the religious right. Picket signs reading "We're here to recruit your children" and "Homosexual Predator" were sarcastic reminders of the scorn that activists in the religious right held for gay and lesbian people, and gay men in particular. At the same time, some Queer Nation members enjoyed toying with the idea that their lives might have as morally corrosive an influence as the religious right claimed. Queer National Joe (pseudonym) expressed this sentiment in an interview: "If they want to tell me that I can bring down civilization just by sucking cock, fine; I'll take that power" (interview with author, 1992).

Religious right leaders, however, took these acts of guerrilla theater out of context, stripped them of their satirical content, and presented them to their constituents as the genuine agenda of the lesbian and gay movement as a whole. They used queer activists' acts of ironic defiance as evidence that, although the lesbian and gay movement claimed to want only equal rights, their hidden agenda was to molest children, just as religious right leaders had been claiming all along. This became clear in an interview for this book with a spokesperson for the Coral Ridge Ministries' Center for Reclaiming America in Fort Lauderdale, Florida, a central hub of religious right activism led by Dr. D. James Kennedy. The spokesperson, whom I will call Jacquelyn, did not care to answer my questions about issue selection, framing of activist slogans, and strategies for talking with the press. Rather, she used our time together to try to convince me that the work that her organization does is valid. To prove this, she gave me many news items reporting crimes that had been committed by gay men, studies of domestic violence in lesbian and gay households, anecdotes of people who had successfully "converted" from gay to straight, and so on. Toward the end of the interview, she had her assistant pull from their files an essay entitled "The Homosexual Agenda" by Michael Swift (1987). It was an essay I had read previously, a satirical mockery of the religious right's more strident claims about the lesbian and gay community. It contained numerous allusions to Jonathan Swift's famous satirical essay "A Modest Proposal," not the least of which was the pseudonym of the author. In the essay, the author argues for the systematized recruitment of children by homosexual men, the abolishment of churches, the elimination of families, and the criminalization of heterosexual acts. As Jacquelyn handed me the essay, I resisted the urge to tell her that she and her organization were exactly what the author was poking fun at. Rather, I listened as she explained to me that this paper proved that her organization was necessary, as it proved that recruiting children and undermining marriage was the hidden agenda of the lesbian and gay movement (interview with author, 2000). As Cindy Patton notes (1993, 143–48), this belief in the literal truth of these claims is widespread in religious right organizations.

While the sarcasm of the Queer Nation–style protests was largely lost on members of the religious right, it is unclear what the impact of the theatrical protests was on the general public. The group was likely inspirational and humorous to some and horrifying and offensive to others. Unlike some of the more moderate protests of mainstream lesbian and gay activists, however, the dramatic flair of the Queer Nation protests caught the attention of the news media. Through coverage of protest events, lesbian and gay issues became a more common topic of public debate. The 1990s marked the first time in which politicians were expected to have something to say about lesbian and gay politics, the issue of outing, or the AIDS crisis. This was a major cultural shift in which lesbian and gay issues were part of the everyday, mainstream, and heretofore straight cultural sphere. While Queer Nation may or may not have garnered sympathy for its radical agenda, it made its mark in greater awareness of and heightened visibility for gay and lesbian, and to a much lesser extent queer, communities.

The Religious Right's Response to Queer Nation and ACT UP

While Queer Nation and ACT UP activists were willing to play the role of the menacing homosexual, the religious right was eager to make use of these groups' theatrical protest performances for their own purposes. They used the words and images of their opposing movement to introduce homosexuality to their religious, conservative constituents in the starkest possible terms. They painted the members of the lesbian and gay movement as social deviants and their claims as undermining the social fabric of mainstream America. This battle of symbols and rhetoric was a crucial moment of interaction between these movements, as it was a moment when each side was trying to bring attention to the words and deeds of the other side, perhaps to a greater extent than their own.

Many organizations in the religious right adopted this strategy in one form or another, sending out letters, posting information on websites, and so on. The most successful part of this cultural campaign was a videotape entitled *The Gay Agenda,* which was produced by a small organization that called itself The Report, but which some have claimed to be the Springs of Life Ministry (Colker 1993, A1). This videotape was distributed widely through conservative Protestant evangelical church networks. It featured video footage and photos of Queer Nation and ACT UP protests, spliced with footage from the San Francisco Gay Pride Parade, particularly focusing on the leather costumes of BDSM and sexual role-play communities. The video cuts smoothly from angry protestors shouting to people in leather and spikes spanking each other. Between these images are interviews with those claiming an expertise in homosexuality, such as anti-gay psychiatrist Joseph Nicolosi, who cite questionable statistics on the rate of sexually transmitted disease among gay men and the amount of fecal matter gay men ingest. Finally, ex-gay activist John Paulk offers his testimonial that his personal experience "in the lifestyle" included frequent anonymous sexual encounters, cross-dressing, sadness, and loneliness. (Many in the lesbian and gay movement later de-lighted in Paulk's later being spotted patronizing a gay bar in Washington, D.C., which called into question the effectiveness of sexual conversion ther-apy. See Kirby 2000, 41–44.) The film is a very powerful and effective por-trayal of exactly those elements of the gay community that would be most disturbing to an evangelical Christian audience. Its message is that the real agenda of the lesbian and gay movement is to remove social restrictions on promiscuity, violence, and deviance. The equal rights that lesbian and gay activists agitate for, the film implies, are the first step toward a social chaos embodied by aggressively sexual lesbians and, especially, gay men.

This tactic of repackaging the more radical queer and AIDS activists as threats to morality, presenting them as if they are the norm in the LGBT com-munity, and distributing this version of their opposing movement widely among potential supporters was very successful. Chip Berlet (1998, 262) esti-mates that of all the issues included in fund-raising letters by religious right organizations in the early 1990s, the anti-gay appeals drew the greatest dona-tions. Increasingly, donation requests included stories of the antics of Queer Nation and ACT UP activists. The stories provided ample evidence for Chris-tian supporters that failing to resist the homosexual agenda would cause major disruption in their lives and a huge shift in cultural values about sexuality. Using ACT UP and Queer Nation as representatives of the lesbian and gay movement in general increased the perceived threat of lesbian and gay activism substantially among conservative, evangelical Christian constituents.

In the first few years of the 1990s, then, the anti-gay mobilization of the religious right was heightened. The American public's attention to issues of homosexuality was greater than it had ever been, and opinions about lesbian and gay rights were shifting away from a state of general indifference on the matter to a more polarized debate. For the first time, politicians were expected to take stances on gays in the military, anti-discrimination protections, domes-tic partner benefits, and other lesbian and gay issues (although this had been a long-standing goal of some parts of the lesbian and gay movement, dating back to homophile political clubs of the 1960s and 1970s, such as the Alice B. Toklas Democratic Club in San Francisco). Anti-gay stances were increas-ingly associated with the religious right's general platform of "family values" and, as such, were linked to stances against abortion, for school prayer, and against making condoms and birth control available to youth. Further, anti-gay political stances were becoming associated with an evangelical Christian religious identity. In other words, the ability to hold no opinion on the issue of lesbian and gay rights, a matter that affected only a small proportion of Americans directly, became more difficult over time as these two opposing movements pushed the issue into the public's view.

Anti-Gay Ballot Initiatives

The successful mobilization of large numbers of grassroots religious right followers did result in some new legislative battles. In the early 1990s a number of local groups began to mobilize around anti-gay and other pro-family stances. One tactic in particular caught the attention of lesbian and gay movement activists nationwide: anti-gay ballot initiative measures. Direct democracy options such as ballot initiatives allow citizens to propose legislation without going through state or local legislative branches. By collecting a sufficient number of signatures on a petition, local social movement groups can put legislative measures directly before the voters. In 1992 religious right groups put statewide measures on the ballot in Oregon and Colorado, as well as in numerous cities and counties. The language of these ballot initiatives was similar: they proposed legislation that would make it illegal to protect lesbian and gay people from discrimination. Though the initiatives varied to some degree in their wording, they all proposed to remove the term "sexual orientation" from any existing anti-discrimination legislation and, in many cases, to ban it from any future legislation.

Local anti-gay groups operated independently, often around local, charismatic leaders such as church pastors. However, they were linked to the larger religious right movement. Much of their funding came from larger religious right organizations such as the Christian Coalition. In addition, these groups shared the strategy of the ballot initiative, similar wording in the legislation, as well as a common set of strategies, such as reaching out to conservative African American clergy who agreed with their anti-gay stance. These African American clerics argued that homosexuality was not a "real" civil rights issue like race, a tactic that served to divide communities and imply that equal rights for lesbian and gay people was somehow oppressive or at least insulting to people of color (Dugan 2005, 50–56).

The wording of many of these initiatives was antagonistic. For example, Oregon's 1992 ballot initiative, Measure 9, read:

> All governments in Oregon may not use their monies or properties to promote, encourage or facilitate homosexuality, pedophilia, sadism or masochism. All levels of government, including public education systems, must assist in setting a standard for Oregon's youth which recognizes that these

"behaviors" are "abnormal, wrong, unnatural, and perverse," and they are
to be discouraged and avoided. (Witt and McCorkle 1997, 165)

Regardless of the harshness of the language justifying the legislation, the
legal prohibitions proposed by most of these bills were unprecedented. As
mentioned above, the initiatives generally called for a ban on the term "sexual orientation" in any current or future law. Their passage would not only
have repealed existing anti-discrimination protections, but also would have
prohibited lesbian and gay people from receiving such protections in the
future. In addition, these bills would have affected related legislation, such
as hate-crime measures, same-sex marriage law, domestic-partner benefits,
and so on. In essence, these ballot measures proposed to make it illegal for
the government to legally recognize lesbian and gay citizens as such. In so
doing, these initiatives attempted to use the public's distaste for homosexuality to undermine the lesbian and gay movement's most prominent strategies for social change: legislation and the courts.

To support this set of ballot initiatives, the religious right developed a
rhetorical device that resonated well with a wide audience of voters. The campaign slogan used in all of these initiatives was "No Special Rights" or "Equal
Rights Not Special Rights" (Dugan 2005, 97–100). As Didi Herman documents (1997, 111–36), the religious right's initial frame of morality and sin
did not resonate well with voters outside of their own constituency. To make
their message more persuasive to a wider audience, religious right organizations made a substantial effort to reframe its claims into civil rights language, to train public spokespeople to discuss things without making biblical
references, and to make clear to constituents the difference between talk
within organizations and that with the outside world. When it came to anti-
discrimination protections for lesbians and gay men, this secular, civil rights
frame became "No Special Rights."

The idea that lesbian and gay rights were "special rights" conveyed the
idea that lesbian and gay people were asking for something extra that heterosexual citizens were not getting from the government. However, this phrase
also resonated with white voters who were concerned that race-based affir-
mative action programs gave an unfair advantage to racial minorities. At the
same time, it was also well received by those African American voters who
were concerned that lesbian and gay rights diluted the concept of civil rights,
which they felt should be defined more narrowly (Dugan 2005, 88–91). The
slogan was also difficult to counter, and lesbian and gay activists found themselves debating whether gay rights were, in fact, "special" in some way. Most
activists, however, argued that anti-discrimination protections were not special

rights. Those in the religious right countered that the U.S. constitution protected everyone equally, so there was no need for additional legislation. This last argument was disingenuous, as legal scholarship has documented well the inequalities lesbians and gay men have endured in terms of child custody, inheritance disputes, and workplace and housing discrimination (Pinello 2003). Regardless, it was an effective debating strategy, especially in media settings where sound bites have an advantage over complex evidence (Gitlin 1980).

Local lesbian and gay movement groups in the states and localities where these measures were put on the ballot found themselves quite suddenly on the defensive. In many cases, lesbian and gay community organizations that were more experienced in organizing social gatherings than political campaigns were at the forefront of the battle to protect lesbian and gay rights. National lesbian and gay movement organizations offered some support, though their financial resources were no match for the religious right's deep coffers. In some cases, there was little agreement within the lesbian and gay community regarding which organization should take the lead in putting together a campaign to defeat the proposed initiatives, causing the lesbian and gay movement to be distracted by infighting and turf wars.

Nor was there agreement on the strategy. In Oregon, for example, some lesbian and gay movement activists wanted to adopt a "we're just like you" campaign, which focused on white, middle-class lesbians and gay men in families with children, and appealed to voters on the basis of sameness. Others, however, wanted to acknowledge the diversity of the lesbian and gay community in the campaign literature and to focus on the discrimination that lesbian and gay people experience, which would appeal to voters on the basis of difference. Although these two sides did not totally reconcile over the course of the campaign, more resources were mobilized for the "sameness" strategy, which was prominent throughout the campaign. In Cincinnati this dispute led to the resignation of one organization's executive director, who was deemed "too militant" as a butch lesbian to lead this fight against the religious right (Dugan 2005, 62–64).

This split over tactical choices mirrored the larger schisms in the lesbian and gay movement discussed above. In particular, the criticism that Queer Nation activists made of the national organizations' failure to be inclusive was felt strongly in these state and local campaigns. While the big organizations made statements indicating that they agreed in principle with the idea of inclusivity, and even took actions such as sponsoring workshops on inclusivity and so forth, the fact remains that even now middle-class whites continue to be overrepresented among the leadership and constituents of these organizations, and that transgender people and bisexuals are not at the fore-front of these organizations' agendas. Although it is relatively easy to agree with the idea of inclusivity, a political contest such as a local ballot initiative really brings into relief the political costs of an inclusive strategy, particularly when the movement wants to project an image of the lesbian and gay com-munity that is palatable to a majority of voters. Where racism, anti-gay prej-udice, and discomfort with nontraditional gender roles are pervasive, leading with diversity will certainly not accomplish short-term electoral goals. How-ever, hiding a community's diversity may reinforce these biases in the long run.

Kim Dugan's analysis of the 1993 Issue 3 campaign in Cincinnati, Ohio, provides an excellent example of this disorganization and lack of consensus. The anti-gay side vetted the wording of their proposals, strategies, and "No Special Rights" slogan through the religious right's various organizational re-sources, such as political analysts, citizen focus groups, and experienced activist leadership. In contrast, the lesbian and gay movement's strategies were ad hoc and uncoordinated. Dugan argues that this led lesbian and gay activists to produce a campaign that did not resonate well with the voters. For exam-ple, one advertising poster offered photos of Adolf Hitler, a hooded Ku Klux Klansman, and Senator Joseph McCarthy, with the simple slogan "Vote No Never Again On Issue 3" (Dugan 2005, 81). Dugan's analysis claims that posters like this one only served to confuse and alienate voters, rather than motivate them to reject the measure. Cincinnati's Issue 3 was passed by the voters, with 62 percent support.

These state and local anti-gay ballot initiatives mobilized many for whom gay rights was formerly a non-issue. Arlene Stein's (2001) portrait of a small Oregon town divided over such a measure is a case in point. Regardless of the fact that very few aspects of anti-gay discrimination are adjudicated at the local level (and thus that the proposed bill was more powerful symbolically than legally), the initiative split the town, with most people aligning with one side or the other. As Stein notes, many of these divisions corresponded to existing social divisions, especially class. In the context of the decline of the lumber industry and the immigration of "outsiders" from the Califor-nian middle class, the proposed anti-gay legislation became a symbol of old, working-class, Oregonian values, a statement of defiance against recent social changes. As such, people on both sides of the issue, regardless of how much they would be affected by the proposed legislation, felt strongly about their support or opposition for the measure.

In attempts to sway voters' opinions and publicize the ballot initiative, there were protests and counterprotests in many places during this period. In some cases protestors with picket signs and bullhorns organized on one street corner while activists on the other side of the issue formed a counter-protest on the other side of the street in response. Radio talk shows featured callers on both sides of the issue, and newspapers ran letters from citizens that debated the legislation. Despite this interaction, there was little real communication between the opposing movements during these ballot initiative campaigns. For the most part, each side talked past the other, using a different body of evidence and appealing to voters on a different set of issues. While one side talked about wanting protection from discrimination, the other side talked about the dangers of child molestation. Some of this public discussion of the issue devolved into hate and even violence. For example, some radio callers claimed that homosexuals should be executed. Lesbian and gay organizations were vandalized and leaders were threatened. The legislation aroused anti-gay feelings in the public, and acts of anti-gay violence increased in areas where these measures were introduced (Berlet and Lyons 2000, 237).

In the end, many of the ballot initiatives were successful. Approximately seventy-five cities and counties in the United States approved them (Galvin 1993, 2904). In Oregon the 1992 statewide initiative, Ballot Measure 9, was narrowly defeated due to opposition among urbanites, despite widespread support throughout the state's rural areas. By 1994, however, similar measures were passed throughout the state at the local and county levels. Idaho faced a statewide measure in 1994 that was narrowly defeated by only a few thousand votes, and Maine's 1995 Question One had a similar fate (Galvin 1993, 2904). As discussed above, Cincinnati's measure was passed by the voters, indicating that these anti-gay initiatives could also be successful in urban areas. Colorado's initiative, Amendment 2, was passed by the voters by a 54 to 46 percent margin. This legislation amended the state's constitution to permanently exclude sexual orientation protections.

The constitutionality of Amendment 2 was challenged in court, with the support of the lesbian and gay movement legal organization, Lambda Legal Defense, as well as the ACLU. In 1996 the U.S. Supreme Court ruled that this amendment was unconstitutional (*Romer v. Evans,* 507 U.S. 620, 1996). This ruling was a strike against the many local initiatives that had passed in the meantime. However, differences in language among the laws left room for further challenges. For example, Cincinnati's Issue 3 was remanded to the Federal Appeals Court at the time of the *Romer v. Evans* decision, and its constitutionality was upheld. The Supreme Court refused to hear an appeal, and this measure stood as law in Cincinnati until a subsequent voter referendum repealed it (Donovan, Wenzel, and Bowler 2000, 181–82). Nonetheless, the Supreme Court ruling temporarily halted the ballot initiative tactic in the religious right's repertoire. Instead, the religious right returned its attention to Republican Party politics and developing new tactics, which I discuss in the following chapter.

Opposing Movements and Issue Selection

The 1996 Supreme Court ruling could easily be interpreted as a victory for the lesbian and gay movement; indeed, many activists celebrated it as such. However, such an interpretation would miss the important fact that keeping lesbian and gay people as a group eligible for anti-discrimination protection was never an issue on the agenda of the lesbian and gay movement. Rather, it was simply a given, a starting place from which fights for such protections as well as other agenda priorities were developed. Nonetheless, lesbian and gay movement organizations dedicated large amounts of time, energy, and resources to these legislative battles, both locally and nationally, making it a top priority for the movement as a whole. During this time, other agenda items were necessarily pushed to the back burner to wait until a better time to introduce legislation, lobby politicians, and so forth.

The introduction of a spray of ballot initiatives over a relatively short period of time highlights the role of opposing movements in setting agendas and in selecting the issue that requires focus at a given point in time. As I argue in chapter 4, the lack of control over issue selection is a common complaint among lesbian and gay movement leaders. For example, Sean Cahill of the National Gay and Lesbian Task Force shows the conflict faced by activists who want to set their own agenda, yet acknowledges the response called for by ballot initiatives: "One of our problems is we don't want to be overly reactive to the anti-gay movement. We don't want them to set the agenda or to set our work plan excessively. [But if an issue] gets on the ballot then we'll have to figure out a way to support the activists who are going to try to defeat it" (interview with author, 2002).

In the absence of opposing movements, impediments to total control over issue selection still exist. For example, factors such as shifting political opportunities, levels of public support, resource limitations, and election cycles often influence which issue movement leaders can prioritize. However, the ability to set the agenda for a movement, or even for a movement organization, is particularly difficult when there is an opposing movement. This is especially true when the resources of one movement vastly outpace those of the other, as is the case in the relative strength of the religious right and the lesbian and gay movement.

Even in the absence of large resource disparities between one social movement and its opponent, this case suggests that another important way that opposing movements can affect the issue priorities of the other is by shifting the venue in which a particular battle is fought. As Meyer and Staggenborg propose (1996), venue shifts can alter the political context in which a particular form of activism is contested. In this case, the use of ballot initiatives relocated the question of anti-discrimination protection for lesbians and gay men away from local governing boards and state legislatures to popular votes, just as it had in the years when Anita Bryant's organization used this tactic. Such a shift introduces a number of strategic issues for a social movement organization to address. For example, the existing support for a particular bill may shift dramatically. In addition, the resources required to convince an audience to support a piece of legislation can differ greatly depending on the venue. A county board of supervisors, for example, might give a social movement organization ten or twenty minutes to make its case. It might review data and written arguments, or commission a study. In a public vote, however, most communication with the voters occurs through media outlets that discourage lengthy discussions and debates. Further, the costs to reach voters through newspaper advertisements, billboards, flyers, or television and radio ads can be out of the reach of a social movement organization. Geographic spread adds further to the cost increase when a venue is shifted from a legislative body to a mass public.

Given the state of public opinion of homosexuality, lesbian and gay movement activists would prefer to keep gay rights legislation out of the hands of the mass public. The opposite is true for the religious right. In city councils, as well as in federal and state legislative bodies, lesbian and gay movement activists can identify a small number of political elites to convince of the merits of their proposed legislation. They will likely have more time to make a case and present the full body of evidence about discrimination against lesbians and gay men and, like any lobbying group, can invest time and energy into fostering connections with lawmakers. Thus, it is not surprising that gay rights ordinances had much more success in legislative bodies than through ballot initiatives (Werum and Winders 2001). The religious right, of course, had the opposite goal. By shifting the political venue in which gay rights decisions were made, they successfully challenged several gay rights measures. Even where anti-gay ballot initiatives were defeated, the election pulled lesbian and gay movement activists into fights that they would rather not be in.

6
Culture Wars:
Battles for the Hearts and Minds of America

The Republican National Convention, the referenda campaigns in Oregon and Colorado, the hyperactivity of God Squad demagogues like Pat Robertson and Lou Sheldon, all these have placed us close to the center of the nation's consciousness.

—John D'Emilio, gay activist and historian, 1992

As historian John D'Emilio notes (2002, ix), "in the 1990s, the world finally did turn and notice the gay folks in its midst." This sea change, in which gay and lesbian lives became visible to a much wider swath of Americans, D'Emilio claims, was dramatic and irreversible. Representations of lesbians and gay men became increasingly apparent in mainstream cultural venues, and public discourse around sexual identity and lesbian and gay rights increased greatly. As the religious right and the lesbian and gay movements' activism continued to gain influence, politicians began to adopt pro-gay or anti-gay positions, and political parties added planks on lesbian and gay rights to their platforms.

Discussions of homosexuality also emerged within churches and religious denominations, where religious teachings about the sin of homosexuality conflicted with moral commitments to welcoming all worshipers. Both church leaders and members alike put considerable effort into forming their opinions, understanding the opinions of others, and attempting to convince one another. People tried hard to reconcile a godly existence with a lesbian or gay life, and they struggled to create ways to allow church participation of lesbians and gay men without reversing their concept that homosexual sex was sinful (see, for example, Moon 2004).

Mainstream media sources also became a venue for debates on homosexuality. Although some portrayals of homosexuality had been present in film and television for decades (Russo 1987), the lives of lesbian and gay fictional characters became increasingly visible over the 1990s. These portrayals were often controversial at first, but over time they became part of the normal landscape of film and television, especially as cable and satellite options added dozens, or even hundreds, of channels to the standard broadcast offerings. Daytime television talk shows also began to feature lesbian and gay characters, followed by bisexual, transsexual, and transgender people (J. Gamson 1998). The popular series *Melrose Place* had a central gay character, and the sitcom *Roseanne* had lesbian, gay, and bisexual characters in minor roles, and even allowed Roseanne to have an exploratory kiss with another woman in 1994 (Walters 2001, 68–72).

It was Ellen DeGeneres's sitcom, *Ellen,* however, that brought a great deal of public attention to the issue in 1997. Perhaps because the actress came out of the closet as a lesbian shortly before the character she played on the show did the same, this show drew protests from religious right groups, sparked debate on talk shows, and even merited news reports. Eventually the show was canceled, but another gay-themed show, *Will and Grace,* about a gay man and his friend, a straight woman, began a long run as a successful prime-time sitcom. These fictional portrayals became one of the ways that people made sense of the politics of homosexuality, normalizing and legitimating lesbian and gay lives (although, critics rightly note, these shows offer a distorted view of lesbian and gay lives).

In the political arena, battles over policy mounted in, as Pat Buchanan put it, the culture war "for the soul of America" (Buchanan 1992, 2544). Despite the fact that this was a polarizing debate, the flurry of activity by opposing movements in the 1990s brought lesbian and gay issues from the margins of political discourse to the center. In the contests over the hearts and minds of the American people, the stakes were as much over symbols as policies. Many policy fights would be decided according to whether Americans saw themselves as an inclusive, diverse group, as the lesbian and gay movement hoped, or as traditionally moral, as the religious right desired. Battles between the religious right and the lesbian and gay movement pushed talk into the public sphere and provoked a broad range of people to think harder about lesbian and gay issues. Poll data indicate that opinions on homosexuality, stable over long periods of time, began to change in the 1990s (see, for example, Loftus 2001; Persell, Green, and Gurevich 2001; Yang 1997). Politicians were questioned directly about their stances on lesbian and gay issues, and they stopped dodging the issue and began to take sides.

These cultural changes were happening in the context of two polarizing opposing movements, each of which pushed its views into the public sphere, yet in so doing confronted the views of its opponent. Changing culture is part and parcel of the work that social movements do (Bernstein 1997; Calhoun 1994). Constructing collective identities, reframing issues, formulating challenges, creating sound bites, and so forth are all central to the social change agenda of many social movements. Thomas R. Rochon argues that social movements are critical agents of cultural change, in the best position to connect claims with group identities (Rochon 1998). In the case of the lesbian and gay movement, years of work framing claims in terms of equality, rights, and justice (to counter earlier frames of mental illness, sin, and deviance) was a necessary foundation upon which the incorporation of lesbian and gay characters in the mainstream media rested. However, the religious right was also, perhaps ironically, useful in harnessing their much greater resources to broadcast the activism of their lesbian and gay opponents to a wider public. And while the intention of the religious right was to deny lesbian and gay claims, their activism played a role in fostering the cultural change that made lesbian and gay lives visible in the 1990s.

In her analysis of the 1993 debate around the New York City Department of Education's proposed curriculum "Children of the Rainbow," which included a book featuring a child with two mothers and another book about kids with a gay father, Janice Irvine (2002) notes that those who fought to exclude lesbian and gay materials from the curriculum produced far more talk about sex than the curriculum itself would have done. This being the largest public school system in the nation, the number of people involved in the debate, the media coverage, and the general public attention to the issues was immense. Nonetheless, in terms of content, the fight over the rainbow curriculum mirrored debates over whether lesbian and gay lives should be acknowledged that were going on in any number of school boards across the country (see also Fields 2008; Luker 2007). In the end, opponents of the rainbow curriculum won, and it was shelved. Regardless, over the course of the debates, talk about lesbian and gay families was broadcast across the city as well as the nation, creating a surge of public discourse on the topic.

Irvine's insight can be applied broadly to the ongoing activism of the religious right and the lesbian and gay movement. While the religious right's agenda has been to exclude lesbian and gay people from social institutions like education, the military, and marriage, in an attempt to build a nation in which lesbian and gay voices are not reflected in legitimate public discourse, their activism increased visibility of gay men and lesbians by producing public discourse about their lives. This dynamic is evident from the earliest days of anti-gay activism and has continued throughout the decades. Each of these opposing movements has produced a good deal of talk about lesbian and gay issues in the course of their activism. That said, with their superior financial and media resources, the religious right was able to pose multiple challenges across a number of political venues, perhaps playing an even bigger role in producing public discourse about lesbian and gay lives than the lesbian and gay movement itself.

Lesbian and Gay Movement-Produced Discourse

The lesbian and gay movement successfully pushed a number of issues from its agenda into the public sphere over the course of the 1990s. Having experienced significant movement growth and established several large national organizations, the lesbian and gay movement had unprecedented access to political elites at the national level. Political allies became more numerous, and the presidential election held great promise for this movement, as Bill Clinton had campaigned openly for lesbian and gay rights. As promised, Clinton placed several lesbian and gay movement activists into prominent positions in his administration. In addition, Clinton issued a ban on discrimination based on sexual orientation for all federal employees through executive order. He also increased funding for HIV research and services substantially, although some maintain that the increases were not enough (Rimmerman 2000b). Clinton also supported the Employment Non-Discrimination Act (ENDA), a narrow lesbian and gay rights bill that would have prevented discrimination in employment, but not housing or public accommodations. The bill was defeated in Senate in 1997 by a vote of 49–50 (Bull 1997, 40–42).

Of all of the Clinton-related policy challenges, however, none captured the attention of the public as much as the debate over Clinton's promise to issue an executive order removing the ban on lesbians and gay men from serving in the armed forces. The religious right mobilized early in Clinton's term to expose his plan to issue this order, rallying the support of military insiders, key Republican Senators and veterans' groups (Rimmerman 2000b, 47). All of these parties claimed that the military could not function well with lesbians and gay men in their ranks. The right-wing frame for this debate implied that the military was currently free from lesbians and gay men and that the change in policy would disrupt this exclusively heterosexual social institution, destroying morale among servicemen and women. The lesbian and gay movement knew that lesbians and gay men had been serving in the military for decades while remaining in the closet, enduring great personal risk to serve their country (see, for example, Bérubé 1990).

This debate concluded with a compromise policy, known as "Don't Ask, Don't Tell, Don't Pursue." Neither the religious right nor the lesbian and gay movement saw this policy as a victory, but it was a particularly substantial blow to lesbian and gay movement activists' morale. Before Clinton's campaign promises to lift this ban, it was not a high priority item on the lesbian and gay movement's agenda. Instead, it was seen by many as potentially the first small step toward widespread progress on lesbian and gay rights in general. They found, however, that this small step, policy-wise, was a profound symbolic challenge. As such, members of the right wing, led by the charge of religious right activists, put up a very strong fight and brought the debate over lesbian and gay rights to the center of Americans' attention.

In addition to these federal-level policies, the lesbian and gay movement introduced a number of policy proposals at the state and local levels, and continued their activism in the courts. Challenges over sodomy laws, hate crimes legislation, and discrimination protection put forth by lesbian and gay movement activists at state and local levels increased dramatically through the 1990s, creating several hundred occasions for public debate over lesbian and gay rights (Werum and Winders 2001). Yet, the policy contests would not have received near as much debate if they had not been amplified by the religious right, whose vast resources and access to media outlets are unparalleled.

Religious Right-Produced Discourse

The religious right's massive resource base, its infrastructure of church networks, and its access to media—both its own outlets and mainstream news media—have contributed to an array of debates over a number of issues in the pro-family platform, including lesbian and gay rights. Over the course of the 1990s, the religious right also had unprecedented access to the political sphere and introduced a number of legislative issues; the state and local ballot initiatives discussed in chapter 5 are among the examples. There were a number of state and local challenges to lesbian and gay rights introduced by religious right organizations—including sodomy statutes that specifically criminalized same-sex sexual contact—and limits on child custody, adoption, and foster care by lesbians and gay men. In addition, the religious right promoted several national-level challenges that further increased public discourse about lesbian and gay lives.

National Endowment for the Arts

The religious right was able to mobilize its resources to produce controversy, even over somewhat mundane bureaucratic processes, such as in their battle

with the National Endowment for the Arts (NEA), the federal agency responsible for supporting a variety of artistic endeavors. This program became a
target of the religious right throughout the 1990s. Leaders in the religious right
wanted a much narrower version of art, one that aligned with conservative,
evangelical Christian morality, to guide the funding decisions of the agency.
The battle against the NEA became a battle over a nation's values, as it challenged the government's role in supporting diversity of artistic expression,
especially for artistic projects that subvert social norms. Holding up particular pieces of art as obscene, immoral, or offensive, the religious right questioned the legitimacy of the NEA altogether.

Lesbian and gay themes were prominent among those artworks that the
religious right claimed to be offensive. For example, the photographs of gay
artist Robert Mapplethorpe, which included sexually explicit imagery, and
Tongues Untied, an autobiographical documentary film by gay, HIV-positive
director Marlon Riggs, were foremost among those condemned by conservative activists, as were artworks they considered blasphemous, such as Andres
Serrano's 1987 photograph of a plastic crucifix submerged in urine, *Piss Christ.*
Religious right activists in the American Family Association began lobbying
Congress to defund the NEA as early as 1989. Although they were not initially successful in either dismantling the NEA or reducing its budget, their
actions were sufficient to cause concern among the NEA's leadership. In 1990
the agency's chair, John E. Frohnmayer, vetoed grants to four artists whose
work had passed through the agency's peer-review process due to his concern that the works would draw the wrath of conservatives. Frohnmayer eventually resigned under the political pressure around the incident, and the "NEA
Four" later sued and won money equal to the amounts of the grants they were
denied (Honan 1992).

Over time, however, the religious right did have some success in reducing the budget of the NEA. Over several years in the 1990s the NEA was
repeatedly targeted for budget cuts, and it suffered numerous Republican-led
attempts to dissolve the organization altogether. The lesbian and gay movement, whose advocates knew that the public was uneasy with explicit sexuality, expressed its opposition through meetings with NEA leaders and press
releases, rather than through a more public campaign. Although the NEA was
not dissolved, and over time its budget was brought back to earlier levels,
concerns about sexuality in publicly funded art remain. These concerns have
spilled over into scientific research as well, as the major federal funding sources,
the National Science Foundation and the National Institutes of Health, have
been under special congressional scrutiny for projects that are related to sexuality and sexual behavior (Agres 2003).

Consumer Boycotts

The religious right also used consumer boycotts to pressure policy changes within a number of corporations. Recent scholarship suggests that boycotts and other protests can, under some circumstances, affect the stock prices of publicly traded companies, giving managers and boards of directors a reason to pay attention to their claims (King and Soule 2007). They can create undesired negative public attention and damage a company's reputation. Boycotts require very few resources from activists and thus are common protest tactics. It remains unclear, however, whether this tactic is effective at producing policy change within the targeted organizations. Nonetheless, the religious right used boycott tactics liberally throughout the 1990s.

The American Family Association (AFA) was a religious right organization that was particularly active in promoting boycotts during this period. The AFA called for boycotts of numerous organizations that supported lesbian and gay rights, offered benefits to domestic partners of lesbian and gay employees, or advertised to lesbian and gay niche markets. They encouraged members to boycott Volkswagen, Microsoft, and American Airlines on these grounds. The most widely publicized of these efforts, however, was the 1996 boycott of the Walt Disney Corporation, which included their amusement parks, Disneyland and Walt Disney World, as well as its numerous entertainment companies such as Miramax Films and ABC Television. Disney offers domestic partner benefits to its employees and has non-discrimination policies that include sexual orientation. Its major offense in the eyes of the AFA, however, was its annual "Gay and Lesbian Day" at its theme parks. The Disney boycott was joined by the Southern Baptist Convention in 1997. Disney ignored the boycott, refusing to change either its human resources or its theme park policies, and it did not appear to suffer any negative consequences. The boycott was rescinded in 2005.

The lesbian and gay movement also called for boycotts in this period. Two in particular garnered the attention of news media. The first of these was a 1991 boycott of a chain restaurant, Cracker Barrel, in response to the company's firing an employee because he was "obviously" gay, as well as its formal, written policy of purging gay employees from its personnel (NGLTF 2007a). The company responded to the claims of discrimination by announcing that it would rescind its discriminatory policy, though the written policy remained unchanged and the employee in question was not rehired. The company did adopt a non-discrimination statement that included sexual orientation over a decade later, which lesbian and gay movement groups claimed as a victory, but the boycott's impact on the board's decision is questionable.

The second boycott involved the entire state of Colorado, in response to its adoption in 1992 of the anti-gay ballot initiative, Amendment 2. The National Gay and Lesbian Task Force, in coalition with a number of other groups, recommended that all business and leisure travel to Colorado be suspended. This boycott seemed largely a symbolic protest, since the amendment's reversal would have required another ballot initiative, which was unlikely. However, some activists suggested that the boycott was a warning to other states considering similar ballot initiatives (Schleder 1994). As Amendment 2 was struck down by the U.S. Supreme Court in 1996, this boycott was in place for almost four years.

Overall, the boycotts from either side did little to promote policy change. However, they may have been useful tools to generate media attention or to mobilize constituents. In addition, the boycotts can be seen as cultural challenges, attempts to wage symbolic battles for the sympathies of various publics. Indeed, activist organizations are hard pressed not to take a public stand in opposition to actions that are in conflict with their organizational goals, and a boycott is a low-cost option to make a symbolic claim in one arena while continuing less public or higher priority work in other issue areas. It is unclear what effect, if any, the boycotts had on public opinion over this decade on either side of the issue.

Sexual Conversion Therapy

In 1998 the religious right led a campaign to challenge lesbian and gay identity directly in their promotion of sexual conversion therapy. Sexual conversion therapy refers to a wide variety of programs that consider homosexuality a psychological disorder and seek to "cure" lesbians and gay men of it (Robinson and Spivey 2007, 651). These programs range from charismatic church meetings where the demons of homosexuality are exorcised from attendees to live-in retreats in which total withdrawal from the lesbian and gay subculture can be achieved. Those promoting this therapy claim that the successfully treated person becomes "ex-gay," living a heterosexual lifestyle, free from desire for members of their sex. For the most part, the therapy combines Bible study with gender socialization, and to varying degrees it incorporates some aversion therapy techniques from early psychological treatment of homosexuality. For example, clients might be told to imagine being nauseated when aroused by a homosexual thought or fantasy (Haldeman 1994, 223).

Although some techniques are borrowed from psychology treatments used decades ago (and since discarded), the counselors are seldom psychologists themselves; rather, they are exempt from most professional licensing requirements because they fall under the rubric of religious counseling (Besen

2003, 38). It is unclear how effective sexual conversion therapy is, given the difficulty in measuring homosexuality and the wide variety of "treatment" programs encompassed by the term. The claims of high success rates made by these groups are unsubstantiated, and critics of the groups point to the many so-called ex-ex-gays who later reclaimed their lesbian or gay identities, including a few leaders of these same ex-gay organizations (Besen 2003, 30–39).

For many years, these groups provided services to lesbians and gay men who sought them out, but they largely stayed out of the public sphere and remained uninvolved with political activism. However, this changed in 1998 when several religious right groups established a coalition to promote sexual conversion therapy to the public at large. This group created a major publicity blitz for sexual conversion therapy, publishing a series of full-page advertisements in major newspapers across the United States, which they called the "Truth in Love" campaign. These advertisements publicized sexual conversion therapy's claim to heal homosexuals and featured ex-gay people who gave testimonials of the treatment's effectiveness. The ads denied the existence of an innate lesbian or gay orientation and argued instead that homosexual people were emotionally disturbed and in need of help. The ads encouraged family members and friends of lesbian and gay people to confront them and suggest sexual conversion therapy, framing such interventions as expressions of love. The print advertisements were followed by two television commercials in the same vein. The advertisements brought the news media's attention to the issue of sexual conversion therapy, and several newspapers, news magazines, and television news programs produced stories on the practice, including *Newsweek,* which ran a cover story on two of the movement's leaders, Anne and John Paulk, a married couple who both were formerly homosexual.

These public claims that therapy could cure homosexuality challenged the existence of a lesbian or gay identity, undermining the basis for the lesbian and gay movement's call for anti-discrimination protection and other policy change. It called into question whether lesbians and gay men were a "real" social group deserving of legal protection from discrimination. The ads themselves pointed to the connection between a rejection of lesbian and gay identity and anti-gay political stances: "For years Christians have taken a stand in the public square against aggressive homosexual activism. . . . And we want to share the hope we have in Christ, for those who feel acceptance of homosexuality is their only hope" (Alliance for Traditional Marriage et al. 1998). Without bringing up any particular policy goals, the advertisements argue for a broad stance against any claims to lesbian and gay rights.

Recognizing the political dangers of allowing this framing of homosexuality to stand unchallenged, the lesbian and gay movement immediately responded to the ads. Rather than their usual practice of issuing a press release and calling reporters, the movement responded in kind, with full-page print advertisements in the *USA Today* and the *Washington Times*. The Human Rights Campaign took the lead in coordinating a response with many other organizations, and they quickly produced an ad that disputed many of the claims of the ex-gay ads. They matched the ads stylistically, and they made a bid to associate idealized symbols such as God, family, and America with the lesbian and gay movement as opposed to the religious right (Fetner 2005). The advertisements took significant resources from the lesbian and gay movement, simply in order to reassert its legitimacy in the public sphere. However, at the same time, this campaign also produced a lot of public discourse about lesbian and gay lives, and brought this discussion to a wide audience.

Same-Sex Marriage

The lesbian and gay rights issue that caught the public's attention the most in the 1990s, however, was undoubtedly same-sex marriage. Republican politicians, in particular, took up this issue as a cornerstone of their platforms, while Democrats for the most part struggled to find a stance that would suggest support for equal rights without supporting same-sex marriage itself. The marriage issue generated much legislation at both federal and state levels, through lawmaking and ballot initiatives, as well as myriad challenges through the courts. Most of the policy outcomes of these challenges opposed the legal recognition of same-sex marriage, but not all of them. At the time of writing, one state, Massachusetts, has legalized same-sex marriage and a handful of others have established civil unions and domestic partnerships that are eligible for some of the same statewide benefits as marriages. Outside the United States, a number of countries have legalized same-sex marriage or recognized same-sex relationships legally in some form.

To many, it may have appeared that the push for legislation on same-sex marriage was driven largely by the lesbian and gay movement, but in the early 1990s few lesbian and gay movement organizations were engaged in activism around this issue. There had been a few unsuccessful court cases in which same-sex couples challenged marriage-licensing practices, when one case in Hawaii caught the nation's attention, as well as that of the lesbian and gay movement. In *Baehr v. Lewin* (74 Haw. 530, 852 P.2d 44, 1993) three same-sex couples claimed that the state's refusal to issue marriage licenses to them constituted sex discrimination. While this was not the first such court challenge, it was the first one that looked as if it would be successful. In 1993 the Hawaiian state supreme court ruled that the practice of denying marriage licenses to same-sex couples would be unconstitutional unless the state could provide a "compelling state interest" for it, and it sent the case back to a lower court to give the state an opportunity to make that argument. This heightened test for constitutionality signaled an impending victory for the same-sex couples. Only after the case looked promising did national lesbian and gay movement organizations become involved, with Lambda Legal Defense joining the case as co-counsel. However, the courts would not decide the Hawaiian same-sex marriage issue. The state legislature passed a new law limiting marriage to male-female couples, and the people of Hawaii voted to amend their constitution to make clear that the legislature had the right to impose such a law (Lewis and Edelson 2000, 200).

Up to this point, same-sex marriage had not been a top priority for the lesbian and gay movement. Many in the lesbian and gay community oppose same-sex marriage as a patriarchal, heterosexual institution and point to the success of lesbian and gay communities in establishing a diverse array of relationship types precisely because they do not view their lives through the lens of marriage (see, for example, Ettelbrick 1997). From this perspective, a lesbian and gay movement that fights for same-sex marriage would be inherently assimilationist, doing more harm than good to lesbian and gay communities. Others saw same-sex marriage as an equal rights issue and, indeed, supported an assimilationist track for lesbians and gay men. Rather than spark a major internal debate about marriage within lesbian and gay communities, most lesbian and gay movement organizations simply ignored the issue, putting it on the back burner in light of other priorities such as nondiscrimination ordinances and anti-gay violence. Lesbian and gay activists in the early 1990s might have preferred that this issue not come to the nation's attention at all, given the public's strongly negative opinions of same-sex marriage (Brewer and Wilcox 2005; Lewis and Edelson 2000).

Religious right activists, on the other hand, saw their opposition to same-sex marriage as an issue with strong cultural resonance and popular support. Many leaders in the religious right considered marriage to be a tipping point for conservatives who had not yet joined the movement. The symbolism of changing one of the nation's most cherished and emotionally laden institutions would evoke strong responses from a broad constituency. Religious right arguments focused on the sanctity of marriage as a cultural symbol. From this perspective, to allow two men to marry would be to trample upon a holy gift. The idea of two women or two men marrying each other evoked such passion among conservative, evangelical Christians that the religious right considered this to be an issue worth pursuing.

Pursue it they did, in a massive grassroots mobilization throughout the country. At the federal level the 1996 Defense of Marriage Act (DOMA) was quickly passed by the Senate and the House and signed into law by President Clinton. The law limited the federal definition of marriage to "a legal union between one man and one woman as husband and wife" and freed states from the obligation to recognize the marriages of other states (Pub. L. No. 104-199, 110 Stat. 2419, 1996). Despite this law, two dozen states passed similar legislation in the next two years, followed by more states, for a total of thirty-nine by 2004 (Cahill 2004, 7). In addition, several of these states also amended their constitutions to prevent same-sex marriage, and others passed laws that would forbid not only same-sex marriage, but also recognition of same-sex civil unions or other legal recognition of gay and lesbian partnerships. Almost all of the 1996 Republican presidential candidates signed a pledge to defend marriage against the inclusion of same-sex couples, as politicians all over the country began to denounce the harms of "gay marriage" (Cahill 2004, 81).

Leaders in the religious right may have thought that this issue would be an easy victory, given how important the symbolic aspects of marriage are to many people. This issue indeed mobilized new supporters and invigorated long-term constituents. People have strong feelings about the issue, and public opinion in the early 1990s was clearly opposed to both the idea of same-sex marriage and to changing marriage laws to make them more inclusive (Yang 1997). Without a doubt, this issue has been an effective tool for the religious right in rallying supporters, Republican politicians, and the public alike in opposition to lesbian and gay rights. However, perhaps unexpectedly, this issue has also mobilized the lesbian and gay movement in response, including many lesbian and gay people who had not previously been involved in activism (Pinello 2006).

Dozens of new lesbian and gay movement organizations emerged to fight for same-sex marriage. National organizations began to devote resources to the marriage issue and, to varying degrees, to partnership issues more generally. To a greater extent than ever before, lesbian and gay movement organizations began to frame lesbian and gay rights in terms of relationships and families, rather than just individuals. This shift in movement priorities is especially interesting, given that some of the earliest internal disputes within lesbian and gay organizations, especially in New York City, were the result of lesbians demanding that gay men pay more attention to "women's" issues such as child custody and family issues. Although it took decades to get there, mainstream organizations began to acknowledge the limits of an exclusive focus on individual rights in securing equality for lesbian and gay people.

As the same-sex marriage issue quickly became a top priority for many lesbian and gay movement organizations, they successfully used the courts to make progress (Pinello 2006). On similar grounds to the court case in Hawaii, in 1999 the Vermont state supreme court ruled that the exclusion from marriage was unconstitutional and ordered the legislative branch to amend the law in order to grant the same "benefits and protections that flow from marriage under Vermont Law" (*Baker v. State,* 170 Vt. 194, 1999). While this was indeed a victory for the lesbian and gay movement, the legislature stopped short of legalizing same-sex marriage, opting instead for a different category of relationship, civil unions, that were eligible for state-level benefits equal to married couples. In 2003 the Massachusetts Supreme Judicial Court ruled that it was unconstitutional to bar same-sex couples from the institution of marriage, making that state the first, and as of this writing the only, state to grant legal status to same-sex marriages (*Goodridge v. Mass. Department of Health,* 440 Mass. 309, 798 NE2d 941, 2003). Nine other states have some form of legal recognition of same-sex partnerships (NGLTF 2007b).

The lesbian and gay movement has mobilized many new constituents around this issue. They have also found allies in a number of bureaucrats and elected officials who have been willing to commit public acts of civil disobedience to grant marriage licenses to same-sex couples and perform same-sex wedding ceremonies. The most publicized case was the San Francisco mayor, Gavin Newsom, who defied California's state DOMA law, which restricted marriage to one man and one woman, and ordered the county clerk to issue marriage licenses to same-sex couples and perform official wedding ceremonies. More than four thousand marriage licenses were issued before the state supreme court ordered the city to cease issuing licenses, later ruling the marriages void (Egelko 2004). County officials in New York, New Mexico, and Oregon have issued marriage licenses to same-sex couples as well.

While it is evident that the lesbian and gay movement has mobilized successfully around the issue of same-sex marriage, it would be a mistake to conclude that this movement took the lead in pushing the marriage issue from the start. Lesbian and gay organizations knew well that Americans strongly oppose same-sex marriage, and most made the strategic decision to give the issue a low priority, despite the negative impact that exclusion from marriage has on some lesbian and gay people's lives. For example, many are not eligible for the health benefits provided by their partner's employer. Some are denied inheritances upon their partner's death. Others cannot claim partner's pensions, and none are eligible to collect social security benefits of deceased partners, which are provided to legal spouses.

It is a much more historically accurate account to claim that the lesbian and gay movement was pulled into the same-sex marriage battle by the religious right's massive campaign to reinforce the legal exclusion of same-sex couples from marriage that had already existed throughout the United States. The religious right's confidence in its success on this issue, supported by public opinion data, appears to be crumbling, however, in the face of the few court decisions that have favored same-sex marriage. Despite securing legislative victories at the federal level, as well as in two-thirds of states, religious right activists continue to push for the Federal Marriage Amendment, an amendment to the U.S. Constitution. This tactic reveals a fear that the state and federal DOMAs may eventually be ruled unconstitutional. Adding to these fears is the policy momentum of the international community. A handful of countries, including Canada, have in the past few years changed their laws to legally recognize same-sex marriage, giving lesbian and gay movement activists hope that the tide is turning on this issue. At this point, however, it is unclear what impact the same-sex marriages performed abroad will have in the United States.

Public Opinion

Changing people's minds about homosexuality and lesbian and gay rights has been a key cultural goal for each of these social movements throughout their history. Many social movements organize their activism to encourage the public to consider their issue and to change people's minds. On the one hand, having greater public support may make it more likely that a movement's policy proposals will be enacted. On the other hand, changing people's minds is often an end goal in itself: to change the culture to make it more welcoming of a group of people, and to reduce harassment, violence, and discrimination through education (Rochon 1998). It is common to see, in this vein, literature produced by social movement organizations to educate an audience about issues, or press appearances by organization representatives to garner viewers' sympathies. However, this issue is more complicated in the case of opposing movements, when two social movements of different sizes are simultaneously working to affect public opinion in different directions. There has been a great deal of survey data on public opinion about lesbian and gay issues since the 1970s, so it is possible to understand changes in public opinion over time. Controlling for numerous influences on people's opinions, such as gender, marital status, and education, studies of attitudes indicate that there has been a significant increase in tolerance of, if not approval for, homosexuality and lesbian and gay rights (Loftus 2001; Yang 1997). They also indicate that this is genuinely a result of people changing their minds, rather than a side effect of other social changes. For example, scholars have tested whether these changes are simply the result of the public becoming more educated or economically secure (Persell, Green, and

Gurevich 2001), or whether an aging population or a loosening of social mores around sexuality more generally underlies the changes in attitudes (Loftus 2001). However, these studies have determined that the change in attitudes toward homosexuality is independent of these other effects.

These data suggest that the lesbian and gay movement may have been quite successful at changing public opinion. But what of the religious right? On the one hand, this movement has been successful in mobilizing large numbers of constituents. But while they have been very successful at convincing people to participate, this ability to motivate does not appear to have had much effect on public opinion overall. For example, Jelen and Wilcox (2003) argue that attitudes on one of the religious right's top issues, abortion, have changed very little over the last thirty years, despite mass mobilization by social movements on both sides of the issue.

In most cases, changes in public opinion occur slowly over time. Further, most change is not due to individuals changing their minds, but rather to generational shifts in attitudes. The age-stability hypothesis, developed by Alwin and Krosnick (1991), suggests that opinions on controversial social issues are formed by early adulthood, and change little with age. Many studies have confirmed this hypothesis, indicating that on most controversial social issues, change in public opinion over time is largely a consequence of generational differences. As older generations are replaced with younger generations, overall attitudes change, without much change within each cohort (Firebaugh and Davis 1988; Quillan 1996). Survey data indicate, however, that attitudes to homosexuality may be the exception to this rule. Studies that compare the attitudes of people from different age cohorts have found that similar percentages of people of all ages have changed their minds about homosexuality in the past two decades (Treas 2002; Andersen and Fetner 2008). Although younger people are more tolerant of homosexuality than older people, this issue has been unlike others in that it has inspired some people of all ages to change their minds, resulting in increasing acceptance of homosexuality in general and lesbian and gay rights more specifically.

Further, the timing of these changes in opinion suggests that the religious right has not been effective at swaying opinions of large numbers of people. A number of surveys indicate that in the United States, attitudes toward homosexuality remained very negative and more or less steady over the 1970s and 1980s. Then, in the 1990s, attitudes began to change, becoming more approving of homosexuality in dramatic fashion over a short period of time (Loftus 2001; Yang 1997). Of course, it still can be argued that social forces other than social movement activity were at the root of these changes in opinion, and so it is useful to look at attitudes toward homosexuality from a comparative perspective. The World Values Survey allows researchers to do just that, as it asks the same question about homosexuality in a number of countries around the world (Inglehart et al. 2001). My colleague Robert Andersen and I have compared attitudes in two culturally similar countries, the United States and Canada (Andersen and Fetner 2008). Indeed, we found different patterns of changing attitudes toward homosexuality over time. Canada showed a relatively steady increase in tolerance between 1980 and 2000, unlike the United States, which showed steady levels of tolerance through the 1980s and then changing opinion after 1990.

In both nations people became more tolerant of homosexuality at a quite dramatic pace, relative to other sorts of attitudinal change. This suggests that the lesbian and gay movement's efforts to educate and persuade the public to accept homosexuality were successful, while the religious right's anti-gay messages were not. Second, the difference in the timing of these changes in attitudes is also worth considering. Whereas Canadians' attitudes grew more tolerant rather steadily over this period, Americans took longer to begin changing their minds about homosexuality, and then showed a steep liberalizing of attitudes after 1990.

What can account for the difference in timing? Some have argued that the impetus for Americans' change of heart has been the increased visibility of lesbian and gay people in television and film media (see Walters 2001 for a discussion of the political relevance of lesbian and gay visibility in popular culture). This media attention, it has been argued, increases visibility of lesbian and gay people, making them more familiar and reducing public fear of homosexuality. Broadening the scope of the analysis to include Canada, however, undermines these claims, in that Canadians have access to most U.S. films and television shows and are regular consumers of American media. They also shared in the timing of the emergence of the AIDS epidemic in their gay communities, which brought the news media's attention to gay men's lives. In addition, both nations have strong and active lesbian and gay movements.

Overall, the lesbian and gay movement histories of the two countries are similar, so we might expect to see similarities in attitudes toward homosexuality. There have been, however, two key differences: social policy regarding homosexuality and the respective strength of the anti-gay opposing movements in each country. Social policy in support of lesbian and gay rights in Canada traces its roots to the decriminalization of homosexuality in 1967, accompanied by Pierre Trudeau's famous declaration, "the state has no business in the bedrooms of the nation" (quoted in McLaren and McLaren 1986, 9). In the United States, sodomy laws varied by state until 2003, when the U.S. Supreme Court ruled them unconstitutional (*Lawrence v. Texas,* 539 U.S.

558, 2003). Other social policies preventing discrimination against lesbians and gay men in employment, the military, and immigration followed from Canada's 1982 Charter of Rights and Freedoms, creating a much different political history than in the United States, where there was a scattered pattern of wins and losses over lesbian and gay rights issues (M. Smith forthcoming). This change in social policy may be at the root of both Canada's greater overall levels of tolerance to homosexuality and its difference from the United States in terms of the timing of its citizens' changing attitudes toward homosexuality over time (Andersen and Fetner 2008).

The second difference between the two countries, however, is worth considering here. Like the United States, Canada's lesbian and gay movement does face an opposing movement that looks similar to the American religious right. It has adopted the same "pro-family" rhetoric, has similar organizations—often related to U.S. organizations—and draws its support heavily from the conservative, evangelical Christian community. However, unlike in the United States, in Canada this movement is relatively weak (Herman 1994). One might expect that the stronger American religious right would suppress tolerance of homosexuality in the United States; however, the patterns of changing attitudes over time show just the opposite trend. Because the American shift toward more tolerant attitudes was the most pronounced between 1990 and 2000, when the religious right was at its peak of mobilization, publicity, and political success, the data indicate that the religious right did not increase intolerance of homosexuality. If the religious right did convince some people to become less tolerant of homosexuality, these were too few to keep the overall pattern of public opinion from becoming more liberal. In fact, these data suggest that the increase in public discourse sparked by the religious right may have played some role in increasing overall levels of social tolerance for homosexuality in the United States. While these data are insufficient to establish a causal connection, they do lend support to the claim that the religious right's capacity to bring attention to lesbian and gay issues pushed Americans to adopt more tolerant attitudes. More research on this is needed.

Contested Symbols and Public Discourse

Joseph Gusfield (1981) argues that interested parties compete for the ownership of public issues. This means that people with agendas, like activists, bureaucrats, or elected officials, engage in public contests to frame the issue in a way that reflects their world view, supports their desired policy outcomes, or values their ideas. The policy battles discussed above can be viewed as classic ownership struggles, in this case between two movements. Janice Irvine (2002) astutely notes that one of the side effects of ownership battles is increased discourse and public attention to the contested issue. The religious right's massive resource base, its insider status in the Republican Party, and its large number of constituents gave activists in this movement a lot of tools to raise challenges on any number of fronts. Over the course of the 1990s, the religious right did just that. From ballot initiatives to same-sex marriage policies to consumer boycotts and ex-gay therapy, the religious right worked diligently to marginalize lesbian and gay people and to block their inclusion in social institutions. Their diligence in pursuing multiple policy fights in numerous venues produced a considerable amount of policy change: numerous statewide bans on same-sex marriage, the blocking of federal-level anti-discrimination protections for lesbians and gay men, and the continued exclusion of lesbians and gay men from the armed forces. These policy victories are clear. Nonetheless, by tirelessly engaging in this activism, they also produced a great deal of public attention to lesbian and gay public issues.

As I note above, data on public opinion suggest that the activism of the religious right not only failed to convince Americans to denounce homosexuality, but it may have had the opposite effect. The difference between policy and public opinion is, of course, an important one. Improvements in public opinion are by no means guarantees of future policy victories for the lesbian and gay movement, and cultural shifts such as increased visibility do not have the same impact on the lived experiences of lesbians and gay men as policy changes such as anti-discrimination law and same-sex marriage. Nonetheless, cultural goals such as changing people's minds are important goals of social movements, and there has been little attention to the cultural impact of opposing movements. More work on this issue by social movements scholars is needed. In addition to public opinion, the activism of the religious right and the lesbian and gay movement combined to dramatically increase the salience of political issues relating to lesbian and gay rights. By shifting lesbian and gay issues from the margins of political discourse to the center, these opposing movements have created a cultural context in which it is not only acceptable but socially expected to have an opinion on lesbian and gay issues. While it is unclear what this shift in cultural context means for these movements in the future, the cultural battle for the hearts of Americans is moving in favor of the lesbian and gay movement.

7

The Impact of the Religious Right on Lesbian and Gay Activism

We were blessed to have the hateful, bigoted opponents we have had, particularly in the early years before we alone had the clout to push our issues to a vote, let alone center stage.
—Steve Endean, executive director of the Gay Rights National Lobby

In this book I have followed two opposing movements during thirty years of activism. From this longitudinal perspective, it is clear that these movements have ebbed and flowed in concert with each other, the actions of one affecting the choices and the repertoire of the other. The story of these two opposing movements is one of bitterness and angst, of sustained conflict and acrimony. However, it is also a story of movement growth and mobilization, with many moments of success for both sides. Each of these movements has grown exponentially from its early days of grassroots mobilization, and the conflict between opposing movements was one of the factors that promoted this growth. The lesbian and gay movement has struggled for many years and continues to fight for equal rights and full citizenship for lesbians, gay men, bisexuals, and transgender people. Their activism has often been redirected by the religious right over the past thirty years. Yet this battle between opposing movements was not "winner take all," in which one side or the other was the clear victor. Rather, the lesbian and gay movement managed to continue its activism and slowly make inroads to favorable policies, despite the work of the opposing movement. The relationship between these two movements tells us much about the progress of lesbian and gay rights in the United States, as it reveals the dynamics of opposing movement relationships in general.

Looking back over the history of conflict between the religious right and the lesbian and gay movement in the United States, it becomes clear that these movements have maintained an interactive relationship that has affected many aspects of their activism. Not only do these movements fight against each other directly over political issues, but their very claims, and the language and frames they use to make those claims, are determined in part by opposing movement interactions. Similarly, tactical choices such as which issues to take on and which political venues to enter are affected by activists' expectations of responses by their opposing movement. Even organizational structures have been determined in part by the need to compete effectively with opposing movement organizations. Activists on each side have never shied away from featuring their opponent in their fund-raising appeals or in their grievance claims. For activists in each of these movements, their opponents have been useful for mobilization at the same time as they have been a threat to their goals.

Still, it would be a mistake to think that each of these movements had the same sort of effect on the other. The resources of the religious right dramatically outpace those of the lesbian and gay movement. The religious right has several organizations with operating budgets in the hundreds of millions. It has radio, television, film, and print media outlets. It has a vast network of member churches, and it can easily deliver political messages or calls for mobilization to all of the people who attend all of those churches, whether or not they consider themselves activists. On top of that, the religious right has an elite wing of extremely rich and politically powerful donors. It has decision-making power within the Republican Party. All this adds up to a movement size and strength that dwarfs the resources, access, and constituent base of the lesbian and gay movement. Nonetheless, this rich giant of an opposing movement has not stopped the progress of lesbian and gay activists. It has, however, had a significant impact on how those activists have done their work, changing the political and cultural fields in which the lesbian and gay movement is situated. This book has identified a number of ways that the religious right has affected the activism of the lesbian and gay movement.

Social Movements Theory and Opposing Movements

Social movements scholarship makes clear the complexities of understanding how social movements work and how they adjust to changing circumstances. This work has identified at least four broad categories of variables that are relevant to social movements: (1) resources, including money, volunteers, and connections to elites; (2) political contexts, a broad category of various aspects of the political landscape; (3) cultural factors such as framing processes, but also including public opinion and media coverage; and (4) emotional dynamics among constituents and various audiences, including elected officials or other stakeholders.

Each of these categories contains a large number of variables that capture some piece of information relevant to social movement activity. For example, membership statistics would capture one sort of resource for a social movement organization; connections to political insiders would be another. Social movements scholars use these pieces of information to develop insights about how social movements contribute to social change. In the case of opposing movements, each movement can vary along each of these dimensions, adding an order of complexity. Further, different organizations within each movement can similarly vary along these axes. Because opposing movements are in a dynamic relationship, their actions, frames, identities, and so on will have an impact on the experiences of the other movement. To think that activists are harnessing their various strengths not only to interact with the state, but also to circumvent the activism of their opposing movement makes the work of lesbian and gay movement activists look like a very complex chess game indeed.

It is also important to keep in mind that not all social movement organizations are equally invested in fighting an opposing movement. Just as the religious right was pulling the lesbian and gay movement into national politics in the 1980s, for example, many small, local grassroots groups did not make major organizational changes, largely ignoring the threat of the religious right. Even among national organizations, some groups, such as the Human Rights Campaign, are more dedicated to responding to statements and actions of the religious right than others that tend to set their agendas independent from opposing movement forces.

The goal of this book has been to understand how the activity of a social movement can affect an opposing movement. One way to approach this is to consider the ways that opposing movements make it more or less likely to achieve the goals of a social movement. In this case the lesbian and gay movement's goal might be to secure legislation prohibiting discrimination against lesbians and gay men. The opposing movement might rally to defeat a proposed bill, or mobilize to repeal that legislation once it is in place. The lesson learned here is that opposing movements can block or reverse social movement gains. Such a view of opposing movements is accurate enough in the short term, but it misses important pieces of the puzzle, especially the dynamics that develop as the opposing movements persist over time. In particular, such a view would obscure the interactive effect between opposing movements: the effect that each movement has on the other, and the impact of that interaction on social movement goals.

To pare down the complexity of this analytical puzzle, I have approached this problem by focusing primarily on the impact that one opposing movement, the religious right, has made on the other, the lesbian and gay movement. In taking this path, I have focused on the way that one movement has influenced the other. However, I also include some evidence here that the impact of these opposing movements works both ways, and that the religious right has responded to the lesbian and gay movement as well. For example, religious right groups incorporated examples from some of the more theatrical protests of ACT UP and Queer Nation activists into their repertoire of persuasive materials in the early 1990s. Activists on both sides have incorporated the threat of their opposing movement into their political claims and mobilizing appeals, both have responded to shifts in the political context created by their opponents, and both have rallied emotional responses from their constituents and made attempts to channel those emotions into activism. However, the primary goal of this book has been to articulate the impact of the religious right on the lesbian and gay movement.

The Impact of Opposing Movements

In laying out the history of these two opposing movements, a number of dynamics emerge as mechanisms through which the religious right affected lesbian and gay activism. In particular, I have identified seven mechanisms through which the religious right has made an impact on the lesbian and gay movement: framing political claims, mobilizing opposing movement resources, promoting change in opposing movement organizations, heightening emotions of lesbian and gay movement activists, diverting the agendas of activists, and shifting the political venues in which policy decisions are made, blocking their progress, and drawing public attention to the lesbian and gay movement. This is not intended to be an exhaustive list of possible ways that one opposing movement influences the other; rather, it is an empirically grounded set of observations about these movements. Taken together, these mechanisms constitute a framework for further analysis of opposing movements. Below, I discuss each mechanism and offer examples from this historical case.

Framing Political Claims

One of the ways that the religious right has changed lesbian and gay activism is by creating new framing opportunities for movement organizations' political claims. Before an opposing movement was present, political claims of lesbian and gay movement organization were upbeat, educational, and inclusive. When an opposing movement emerged, particularly given the harsh rhetoric that it used to describe lesbian and gay people in its claims, lesbian and gay movement activists responded by changing the way they framed their claims. Referring directly to Anita Bryant and John Briggs in their flyers and newsletters, lesbian and gay movement activists used a new frame that captured lesbian and gay people as a threatened minority, adopted an angry tone, and used an "us/them" language that drew the line between supporters and detractors. In addition, lesbian and gay movement organizations took advantage of the new opportunities for press coverage created by the emergence of their opposing movement, increasing their visibility and their capacity for political voice. Activists indicated that there was strong symbolic value in their opposing movement's public statements denouncing homosexuality. Over time, lesbian and gay movement activists included references to the religious right in some cases and not others. The threat of the religious right was added to their rhetorical repertoire, though it was not always invoked.

Mobilizing Resources for Opposing Movement Organizations

The religious right has also aided the lesbian and gay movement in mobilizing resources by presenting a tangible, immediate threat to the rights of lesbian and gay people. When the anti-gay movement emerged, many were afraid that the lesbian and gay movement would be defeated, never to be heard from again. As the earliest grassroots anti-gay organizations were quickly replaced by the large-scale Moral Majority, with its vast resources, charismatic leadership, and a rhetorical frame that resonated with large numbers of Americans, the prospect of taking on such a Goliath was surely daunting for lesbian and gay movement participants. However, the movement did not fold. Far from it: the lesbian and gay movement experienced organizational growth and mobilization of new constituents and resources that it had never seen before. Although the lesbian and gay movement has never stood a chance at amassing a purse the size of most religious right groups, it was able only since the emergence of the opposing movement to operate on more than shoestring budgets and volunteer labor. From the beginning, rather than shrink from the challenges introduced by the religious right, lesbian and gay movement leaders used the specter of the anti-gay "bigots," as they called them, to mobilize additional constituents and donations.

Previous scholarship has identified this relationship between the mobilization patterns of opposing movements. For example, Zald and Useem (1987, 247) claim that opposing movements are embroiled in "loosely coupled" conflict: a dance of decline and growth in which the victories of one movement inspire mobilization in the opposing movement, and vice versa. However, in our case, victories were not necessary to mobilize the other side.

The threat of the opposition's presence in the political sphere was sufficient. Each movement incorporated the threat of the other to bolster its fund-raising and other mobilization efforts. Berlet (1998, 262) claims that the threat of the lesbian and gay movement is routinely used in direct mail fund-raising of religious right organizations. Some analyses of the lesbian and gay movement claim that the emergence of an opposing movement in the late 1970s mobilized gay men and lesbians both to come out of the closet in large numbers and to join the movement (Marcus 1992, 259).

Inspiring Change in Opposing Movement Organizations

Meyer and Staggenborg (1996, 1649) propose that one of the ways social movements will respond to opposing movements' impact on the political contexts in which they operate is by modifying their organizational structures or creating new organizational forms. Such an adjustment is evident in the lesbian and gay movement, especially over the 1980s, when the movement's national organizations grew and became more professionally coordinated. The lesbian and gay movement at the end of the 1980s was dominated by groups with organizational forms that were much different from earlier groups, looking more like corporations than collections of grassroots protestors. Despite significant criticism from lesbian and gay activists who were suspicious of hierarchical organizational structures, these changes were prompted in part by the religious right's increasing influence in federal politics. They also attracted support from constituents who had not been activists in the past. The checkbook model of activism may, as critics assert, institutionalize resistance and distance members from active participation (Skocpol 2003). However, it can also inspire those who support lesbian and gay rights but who do not want or are unable to invest significant amounts of time and energy into social movement participation.

In addition, there is evidence that this influence on organizational form continued into the 1990s, when the religious right carried out ballot initiatives in multiple locations across the country. National lesbian and gay movement organizations, which by then had significant resources, began to focus their attention on regional offices across the country and hold their annual conferences in different locations each year. Local movement groups scrambled to adjust their organizational structures in order to conduct effective campaigns against anti-gay ballot initiatives. This organizational scramble led to more than one change in leadership in lesbian and gay movement organizations, as well as new coalitions being formed among movement organizations (Dugan 2005, 62–64).

Heightened Emotions

Opposing movements can make an enormous impact on one another's emotional repertoire. They can inspire heightened emotions in activists, including outrage and fear (Ginsburg 1989; Goodwin, Jasper, and Polletta 2001). These emotions can be harnessed by activists and channeled into protest activity (Gould 2002). Intense emotions may also promote despair among constituents, however, leading to demobilization and inactivity (Jasper 1998). Movements can also divert their opponents' agenda by fostering emotional reactions among their opponents' constituents. In general, data on the emotional responses of participants in opposing movements are scarce. In this case, however, there is some evidence that the emotional repertoire of lesbian and gay movement activists, as expressed in its claims making, was altered by the emergence of its opposing movement.

An analysis of the political claims of the lesbian and gay movement in the early years of opposing movement activism reveals an emotional shift from upbeat idealism to outrage and anger. The hostile language that the religious right used to describe lesbians and especially gay men in their early years, claiming they were pedophiles and perverts, was later replaced by a focus on lesbian and gay rights and celebrations of traditional, heterosexual marriage in most political discourse of the religious right. Nonetheless, occasionally religious right activists made hostile claims about the perversity of heterosexuality, which could be counted on to inspire anger and outrage among lesbian and gay movement supporters. Lesbian and gay movement activists saw the emotional response to these hateful claims as useful to their mobilization efforts, and they made sure to publicize these statements as evidence of the real feelings of religious right activists. In addition, even opposing movement messages that do not use hostile language can anger opposing movement activists and constituents. For example, the Truth in Love campaign, in which the religious right claimed that lesbians and gay men were in need of psychological care, used a language of love, hope, and concern. Nonetheless, from the perspective of lesbian and gay people, these claims might well inspire anger and outrage. In any case, the passions with which each side speaks of the policies it supports, and the vitriol that each has cast at its opponents, suggests that emotional interplay is particularly salient in opposing movements, and this area begs further study.

Diverted Agendas

Opposing movements divert the agendas of their opponents, complicating the process through which activists decide which grievances to address, which political venues are most likely to produce positive social change, and how to allocate their resources to the various elements of their agenda. By contesting the activism of their opponents and by introducing new contests on other issues, opposing movements can reshuffle the priorities of the other side. Lesbian and gay movement leaders have repeatedly complained that the religious right has limited their ability to set their own organizations' agenda, leading them to follow the opposing movement into contests that for lesbians and gay men are either lower priorities or less likely to be successful. One example of this diversion of the agenda is the 1998 campaign to undermine lesbian and gay movement claims through the advertisement of ex-gay sexual conversion therapy. When the religious right published these full-page newspaper advertisements, the lesbian and gay movement, rather than continue to focus on their own political goals, poured time, energy, and especially money into responding in kind with advertisements that validated the lives and families of lesbian and gay people. In the absence of the opposing movement action, it is unlikely that this is where they would have invested their efforts.

Not only can opposing movements determine which issues will be contested, but they can also choose the political venue in which the contest will take place. In Meyer and Staggenborg's (1996) theoretical framework each opposing movement is a part of the political opportunity structure of the other, and as such it can alter the political landscape in which its opposing movement acts. Opposing movements will each attempt to work in political venues that are to their advantage, using the courts when legislatures are sympathetic to opponents, or using direct democracy venues when public opinion favors their side. Given the lesbian and gay movement's claims for equal rights and the public's relatively negative opinion of homosexuality, the religious right has repeatedly moved policy decisions on lesbian and gay rights away from legislative bodies to popular votes. From its earliest activism, when Anita Bryant's group, Save Our Children, shifted the venue in which an anti-discrimination bill was decided away from county legislators to voters at large, the religious right has been using popular discomfort with sexuality and its intolerance of lesbian and gay people to its advantage.

Another way that venue shifts have come into play is by bringing policy challenges variably to federal, state, and local levels of government. The multiplicity of locations and venues in which policy challenges occur is costly to an opposing movement, bringing into relief the difference in financial resources between the two movements. The religious right has been very influential in selecting issues and in choosing more favorable political venues than its opponent. The lesbian and gay movement, however, has also attempted to shift venues. In particular, organizations brought numerous challenges to the courts, where public opinion is less influential, as in the case of decriminalization of sodomy (Werum and Winder 2001).

Another site of strategic venue shifting has been the interplay of these two opposing movements with the political party system. Over the course of the 1980s the religious right, especially Pat Robertson's groups, the Freedom Council and then the Christian Coalition, made a concerted effort to gain power in the Republican Party. This highly successful political maneuver created a new political insider status for the religious right. In doing so, the religious right pushed lesbian and gay movement activists to focus on increasing their own access to politicians in the Democratic Party. This further promoted the prominence of the large-scale, national organizations in the lesbian and gay movement. While this drive for access was eventually successful, the spoils of these victories were small indeed. Despite unprecedented access to federal political circles, the religious right was only able to achieve a modicum of the policy change it favored. Similarly, the lesbian and gay movement was disappointed by the policy that emerged from its newfound friends in the White House and the Congress. Immediately following the religious right's emergence in the leadership of the GOP, other religious right groups began a wave of ballot initiative drives, shifting political venues once again.

Barriers to Progress

Related to this is the capacity of an opposing movement to block the political progress of its opponent. In particular, the history of these opposing movements suggests that it may be easier for movements to hinder the progress of their opponents than to make positive progress of their own. The religious right has been able to mobilize to block policy victories of the lesbian and gay movement, even when the policy seemed likely to change. For example, when President Clinton set out to use his executive privilege to lift the military's ban on homosexuals, the religious right was able to mobilize their congressional allies to challenge the president's plan, which resulted in retaining the ban through the "Don't Ask, Don't Tell, Don't Pursue" compromise. Similarly, the lesbian and gay movement used the courts to undo the anti-gay ballot initiative that was passed by Colorado voters.

Opposing movements' capacity to block movement progress, combined with their role in mobilizing opposition, has had a paradoxical effect in the case of the religious right and the lesbian and gay movement. Each opposing movement has grown very large in terms of budgets, memberships, and organizational size. This growth, however, has not been matched by policy outcomes, which have been much more measured. After thirty years of activism by these opposing movements, both sides can claim a number of political victories, but neither can say with any surety that they are close to getting what they ultimately want. Despite limited progress toward social change goals, opposing movements leave each other little room to retreat. The threat of losses compels opposing movements to carry on.

Generating Attention

Finally, the religious right has brought a significant amount of public attention to the issues of homosexuality and lesbian and gay rights. This came in the form of news coverage, political debates over ballot initiatives, pundits railing over same-sex marriage, and politicians taking sides on the myriad proposals put forth by each of these opposing movements. As Meyer and Staggenborg suggest (1996, 1642), balancing norms in the news media encourage the publication of stories about opposing movement issues more than other social movement issues. This has been the case since the first instances of anti-gay activism, when Anita Bryant created new opportunities for media coverage that activists in the lesbian and gay movement could not achieve on their own. Later, the furor with which Pat Buchanan railed about the "culture war" in 1992 was intended to mobilize the constituents of the religious right. At the same time, however, it alerted the rest of the country to the agenda of a growing conservative movement and likely caused some people to consider issues like lesbian and gay rights for the first time.

Opinion poll data suggest that the overall effect of the increased attention to the issue of homosexuality was increased tolerance. Although many in the religious right intended to vilify lesbian and gay people and deny their access to equal rights, by escalating the public discussion of homosexuality, they called upon people across the political spectrum to consider their stance on lesbian and gay rights. In this particular case, the overall result was increased tolerance, but this has come amid an increasing polarization on this issue. Even as more and more people feel very strongly pro-gay or anti-gay, there is a growing group of moderates who have become more tolerant of homosexuality and who support equal rights for lesbian and gay people (Yang 1997).

How the Religious Right Shaped Lesbian and Gay Activism

Looking over the history of these two opposing movements, it becomes clear that they are in a relationship. Given that they are inevitably focused on the same policy goals, whether that is supporting their own proposals or fighting against those of their opponent, the activism of these opposing movements has become connected. That is not to imply parity, however. The religious right is much larger and richer in resources than the lesbian and gay movement. Still, the religious right's greater size and strength, its vast media empire, and its strong influence within the Republican Party has not been enough for it to secure the exclusion of lesbian and gay people from anti-discrimination protections or to maintain the criminal status of same-sex sexual activity. The lesbian and gay movement, much larger than it used to be but very small relative to its opposing movement, has been able to block the religious right from obtaining its most ambitious political goals.

Through the decades-long process of political activism that each of these movements has been engaged in, public awareness of lesbian and gay rights has increased. Cultural representations of lesbians and gay men have become both more numerous and more positive. Political discourse and public debate about lesbian and gay rights has become more commonplace, extending throughout the political system from school boards debating sex education curriculums, to states voting on anti-discrimination protections, to congressional and presidential campaigns, where same-sex marriage is a hot-button issue. In the midst of this debate, people's opinions about the acceptability of homosexuality has changed dramatically. Unlike other sorts of attitude change, which happen slowly as less tolerant generations are replaced by younger, more tolerant generations, this issue has caused some people of all ages to change their minds (Andersen and Fetner 2008). Public support for lesbian and gay rights is even stronger (Yang 1997). Comparative data suggest that the activism of the religious right not only failed to dissuade Americans from accepting homosexuality, but it may have had the opposite effect: increasing tolerance in the United States.

The religious right brought both new challenges and new opportunities to the lesbian and gay movement. Just as early lesbian and gay movement leaders realized, the religious right created setbacks in terms of policy reversals, agenda diversions, and resource drains. However, at the same time, the religious right's antagonism mobilized lesbian and gay movement supporters, energized their outrage, and drew unprecedented public attention to their cause. For better or for worse, from the moment Anita Bryant founded the first anti-gay movement organization, the work of lesbian and gay movement activists would become more complex and multidimensional. There was no way that, at the time, they could see the behemoth conservative movement that would develop in the near future to become the religious right. However, they did see that the emergence of this opposing movement, while worrisome, was not all bad news for them. They embraced the new challenge of their opposing movement head on, and indeed the lesbian and gay movement would never be the same.

Works Cited

Abramson, Paul R., John H. Aldrich, and David W. Rohde. 1994. *Change and Continuity in the 1992 Elections.* Washington, D.C.: CQ Press.

Adam, Barry D. 1995 [1987]. *The Rise of a Gay and Lesbian Movement.* New York: Twayne.

Agres, Ted. 2003. "Sex, Drugs, and NIH." *The Scientist,* November 3. http://www .the-scientist.com/article/display/21753.

Alliance for Traditional Marriage–Hawaii, AFA, Americans for Truth about Homosexuality, Center for Reclaiming America, Christian Family Network, Christian Coalition, Citizens for Community Values, Colorado for Family Values, Concerned Women for America, Coral Ridge Ministries, Family First, Liberty Counsel, National Legal Foundation, and Kerusso Ministries. 1998. "Toward Hope and Healing for Homosexuals." *New York Times,* July 13.

Altman, Dennis. 1971. *Homosexual: Oppression and Liberation.* New York: Outerbridge and Dienstfrey.

———. 1986. *AIDS in the Mind of America.* Garden City, New York: Anchor Press.

Alwin, Duane F., and Jon A. Krosnick. 1991. "Aging, Cohorts, and the Stability of Sociopolitical Orientations over the Life Span." *American Journal of Sociology* 97:169–95.

Amenta, Edwin. 2006. *When Movements Matter: The Townsend Plan and the Rise of Social Security.* Princeton: Princeton University Press.

Amenta, Edwin, Bruce G. Carruthers, and Yvonne Zylan, 1992. "A Hero for the Aged? The Townsend Movement, the Political Mediation Model, and U.S. Old-Age Policy, 1934–1950." *American Journal of Sociology* 98:308–39.

Andersen, Robert, and Tina Fetner. 2008. "Birth Cohort and Tolerance of

Homosexuality: Attitudinal Change in Canada and the United States, 1981–2000." *Public Opinion Quarterly* 72.

Andrews, Kenneth T. 2002. "Movement-Countermovement Dynamics and the Emergence of New Institutions: The Case of 'White Flight' Schools in Mississippi." *Social Forces* 80:911–36.

Andriote, John-Manuel. 1999. *Victory Deferred: How AIDS Changed Gay Life in America.* Chicago: University of Chicago Press.

Apostolidis, Paul. 2000. *Stations of the Cross: Adorno and Christian Right Radio.* Durham, N.C.: Duke University Press.

Armstrong, Elizabeth A. 2002. *Forging Gay Identities: Organizing Sexuality in San Francisco, 1950–1994.* Chicago: University of Chicago Press.

Armstrong, Elizabeth A., and Suzanna M. Crage. 2006. "Movements and Memory: The Making of the Stonewall Myth." *American Sociological Review* 71:724–51.

BACABI (Bay Area Coalition against the Briggs Initiative). 1978. *Third World People Unite to Defeat the Briggs Initiative.* Flyer. Gay and Lesbian Historical Society of Northern California, San Francisco. Robert Ferrell box (90–1), BACABI Statements folder.

BAGL (Bay Area Gay Liberation). 1975. *Mass Gay Picket and Teach In.* Flyer. Human Sexuality Collection, Cornell University, Ithaca, N.Y. Collection #7431, box 10, folder 24.

Baker, Ross K. 1993. "Sorting Out and Suiting Up: The Presidential Nominations." In *The Election of 1992: Reports and Interpretations,* edited by Gerald M. Pomper, F. Christopher Arterton, Ross K. Baker, Walter Dean Burnham, Kathleen A. Frankovic, Marjorie Randon Hershey, and Wilson Carey McWilliams, 39–73. Chatham, N.J.: Chatham House Publishers.

Barnett, William P., and Glenn R. Carroll. 1995. "Modeling Internal Organizational Change." *Annual Review of Sociology* 21:217–36.

Beder, Sharon. 1998. "Public Relations' Role in Manufacturing Artificial Grass Roots Coalitions." *Public Relations Quarterly* 43, no. 2:20–23.

Bell, Arthur. 1971. *Dancing the Gay Lib Blues: A Year in the Homosexual Liberation Movement.* New York: Simon and Schuster.

Berlet, Chip. 1998. "Who Is Mediating the Storm? Right-Wing Alternative Information Networks." In *Media, Culture, and the Religious Right,* edited by Linda Kintz and Julia Lesage, 249–73. Minneapolis: University of Minnesota Press.

Berlet, Chip, and Matthew N. Lyons. 2000. *Right-wing Populism in America: Too Close for Comfort.* New York: Guilford Press.

Bernstein, Mary. 1997. "Celebration and Suppression: The Strategic Uses of Identity by the Lesbian and Gay Movement." *American Journal of Sociology* 103:531–65.

Bérubé, Alan. 1990. *Coming Out under Fire: The History of Gay Men and Women in World War II.* New York: Free Press.

Besen, Wayne R. 2003. *Anything but Straight: Unmasking the Scandals and Lies behind the Ex-gay Myth.* New York: Haworth Press.

Blee, Kathleen. 2002. "The Banality of Violence." *Contexts* 1, no. 4:60–61.

Boston, Robert. 1996. *The Most Dangerous Man in America? Pat Robertson and the Rise of the Christian Coalition.* Amherst, N.Y.: Prometheus Books.

Bray, Alan. 1982. *Homosexuality in Renaissance England.* London: Gay Men's Press.

Brewer, Paul R., and Clyde Wilcox. 2005. "The Polls—Trends: Same-sex Marriage and Civil Unions." *Public Opinion Quarterly* 69:599–616.

Bruce, Steve. 1995. "The Inevitable Failure of the New Christian Right." In *The Rapture of Politics: The Christian Right as the United States Approaches the Year 2000,* edited by Steve Bruce, Peter Kivisto, and William H. Swatos Jr., 7–20. New Brunswick, N.J.: Transaction Publishers.

Bryant, Anita. 1977. *The Anita Bryant Story.* Old Tappan, N.J.: Spire Books.

Bryant, Anita, and Bob Green. 1978. *At Any Cost.* Old Tappan, N.J.: Revell.

Buchanan, Pat. 1992. "Republican Convention Address." *Congressional Quarterly Weekly Report,* August 22, 2544.

Bull, Chris. 1992. "The Outing of a Family-Values Congressman: U.S. Representative Jim McCrery's Double Life." *The Advocate,* September 22, 38–45.

———. 1997. "No ENDA in Sight: The Employment Non-Discrimination Act of 1996." *The Advocate,* May 13, 40–42.

Bull, Chris, and John Gallagher. 1996. *Perfect Enemies: The Religious Right, the Gay Movement, and the Politics of the 1990s.* New York: Crown Publishers.

Button, James W., Barbara A. Rienzo, and Kenneth D. Wald. 1997. *Private Lives, Public Conflicts: Battles over Gay Rights in American Communities.* Washington, D.C.: CQ Press.

Cahill, Sean. 2004. *Same-Sex Marriage in the United States: Focus on the Facts.* Lanham, Md.: Lexington Books.

Calhoun, Craig J. 1994. "Social Theory and the Politics of Identity." In *Social Theory and the Politics of Identity,* edited by Craig J. Calhoun, 9–36. Oxford: Blackwell.

Carpenter, Joel A. 1997. *Revive Us Again: The Reawakening of American Fundamentalism.* Oxford: Oxford University Press.

Centers for Disease Control and Prevention. 2001. *HIV/AIDS Surveillance Report* 13, no. 2.

Chauncey, George. 1994. *Gay New York: Gender, Urban Culture, and the Making of the Gay Male World.* New York: BasicBooks.

Clemens, Elisabeth S. 1996. "Organizational Form as Frame: Collective Identity and Political Strategy in the American Labor Movement, 1880–1920." In *Comparative Perspectives on Social Movements: Political Opportunities, Mobilizing Structures, and Cultural Framings,* edited by Doug McAdam, John D. McCarthy, and Mayer N. Zald, 205–26. Cambridge: Cambridge University Press.

CLGR New York (Coalition for Lesbian and Gay Rights). 1977a. *No More Miami's!* Announcement. Lesbian Herstory Archives, Brooklyn. Org. File: CLGR.

———. 1977b. *March on the UN–August 20.* Flyer. International Gay Information Center, Inc., New York Public Library, New York. Ephemera—Organizations, box 3.

———. 1978. *Street Rallies for Gay Rights!* Flyer. Lesbian Herstory Archives, Brooklyn. Org. File: CLGR.

———. 1979. *We Demand Justice!* Flyer. Lesbian Herstory Archives, Brooklyn. Org. File: CLGR.

Clinton, William. 1992. "Acceptance Speech to the Democratic National Convention." New York, July 16. *American Presidency Project,* http://www.presidency.ucsb.edu/shownomination.php?convid=7.

Colker, David. 1993. "Anti-Gay Video Highlights Church's Agenda." *Los Angeles Times.* February 22.

Crew, Louie, ed. 1978. *The Gay Academic.* Palm Springs, Calif.: ETC Publications.

D'Emilio, John. 1983. *Sexual Politics, Sexual Communities: The Making of a Homosexual Minority in the United States, 1940–1970.* Chicago: University of Chicago Press.

———. 1992. *Making Trouble: Essays on Gay History, Politics and the University.* New York: Routledge.

———. 2002. *The World Turned: Essays on Gay History, Politics, and Culture.* Durham, N.C.: Duke University Press.

Diamond, Sara. 1989. *Spiritual Warfare: The Politics of the Christian Right.* Boston: South End Press.

———. 1995. *Roads to Dominion: Right-wing Movements and Political Power in the United States.* New York: Guilford Press.

———. 1998. *Not by Politics Alone: The Enduring Influence of the Christian Right.* New York: Guilford Press.

DiMaggio, Paul J., and Walter W. Powell. 1983. "The Iron Cage Revisited: Institutional Isomorphism and Collective Rationality in Organizational Fields." *American Sociological Review* 48:147–60.

Donovan, Todd, Jim Wenzel, and Shaun Bowler. 2000. "Direct Democracy and Gay Rights Initiatives after *Romer.*" In *The Politics of Gay Rights,* edited by Craig A. Rimmerman, Kenneth D. Wald, and Clyde Wilcox, 161–90. Chicago: University of Chicago Press.

Dreyfuss, Robert. 2004. "Reverend Doomsday." *Rolling Stone,* February 19, 46–50.

Dugan, Kim. 2005. *The Struggle Over Gay, Lesbian and Bisexual Rights.* London: Routledge.

Duggan, Lisa. 1992. "Making It Perfectly Queer." *Socialist Review* 22:11–31.

Egelko, Bob. 2004. "SF Gay Marriages Head to Court." *San Francisco Chronicle,*

December 21, 2004. http://sfgate.com/cgi-bin/article.cgi?file=/c/a/2004/12/21/MNGQCAF5F01.DTL.

Endean, Steve. 2006. *Bringing Lesbian and Gay Rights into the Mainstream: Twenty Years of Progress,* edited by Vicki L. Eaklor. Binghamton, N.Y.: Harrington Park Press.

Epstein, Joseph. 1970. "The Struggle for Sexual Identity." *Harper's Magazine,* September 1, 37–44, 49–51.

Epstein, Steven. 1999. "Gay and Lesbian Movements in the United States: Dilemmas of Identity, Diversity, and Political Strategy." In *The Global Emergence of Gay and Lesbian Politics: National Imprints of a Worldwide Movement,* eds. Barry Adam, Jan Willem Duyvendak, and André Krouwel, 30–90. Philadelphia: Temple University Press.

Ettelbrick, Paula L. 1997. "Since When Is Marriage a Path to Liberation?" In *Same-sex Marriage: The Moral and Legal Debate,* edited by Robert M. Baird and Stuart Rosenbaum, 257–61. New York: Prometheus.

Faderman, Lillian. 1981. *Surpassing the Love of Men.* New York: Morrow.

Fetner, Tina. 2001. "Working Anita Bryant: The Impact of Christian Anti-Gay Activism on Lesbian and Gay Movement Claims." *Social Problems* 48:411–28.

———. 2005. "Ex-gay Rhetoric and the Politics of Sexuality: The Christian Anti-gay/Pro-family Movement's 'Truth in Love' Ad Campaign." *Journal of Homosexuality* 50, no. 1:71–96.

Fields, Jessica. 2008. *Risky Lessons: Sex Education and Social Inequality.* New Brunswick, N.J.: Rutgers University Press.

Firebaugh, Glenn, and Kenneth E. Davis. 1988. "Trends in Antiblack Prejudice, 1972–1984: Region and Cohort Effects." *American Journal of Sociology* 94:251–72.

Foucault, Michel. 1978. *History of Sexuality.* Vol. 1. New York: Vintage Books.

Fox, Daniel M. 1992. "The Politics of HIV Infection: 1989–1990 as Years of Change." In *AIDS: The Making of a Chronic Disease,* edited by Elizabeth Fee and Daniel M. Fox, 125–43. Berkeley: University of California Press.

Frank, Miriam, Marilyn Ziebarth, and Connie Field. 1982. *The Life and Times of Rosie the Riveter: The Story of Three Million Working Women during World War Two.* Emeryville, Calif.: Clarity Educational Products.

Freedman, Estelle B. 2002. *No Turning Back: The History of Feminism and the Future of Women.* New York: Ballantine Books.

Freiberg, Peter, 1985. "Gay Leadership Begins Reassessing Legal and Political Strategies." *The Advocate,* April 2, p. 8.

GAA (Gay Activists' Alliance). 1971. *No Civil Rights Protection.* Flyer. Lesbian Herstory Archives, Brooklyn. Org File: GAA.

———. 1972. Fair employment flyer. Lesbian Herstory Archives, Brooklyn. Org File: GAA.

————. 1974. Flyer protesting police harassment. Collection: Lesbian Herstory Archives, Brooklyn. Org File: GAA.

Galvin, Thomas. 1993. "Local Initiatives Send Signals on National Trends." *CQ Weekly Report.* October 23, 2904.

Gamson, Joshua. 1989. "Silence, Death, and the Invisible Enemy: AIDS Activism and Social Movement 'Newness.'" *Social Problems* 36:351–67.

————. 1995. "Must Identity Movements Self-Destruct? A Queer Dilemma." *Social Problems* 42:390–407.

————. 1998. *Freaks Talk Back: Tabloid Talk Shows and Sexual Nonconformity.* Chicago: University of Chicago Press.

Gamson, William A. 1975. *The Strategy of Social Protest.* Homewood, Ill.: Dorsey Press.

————. 1992. *Talking Politics.* Cambridge: Cambridge University Press.

Gamson, William, and David S. Meyer. 1996. "Framing Political Opportunities." In *Comparative Perspectives on Social Movements: Political Opportunities, Mobilizing Structures, and Cultural Framing,* edited by Doug McAdam, John D. McCarthy, and Mayer N. Zald, 275–90. New York: Cambridge University Press.

Gay, A. Nolder (pseudonym). 1978. *The View from the Closet: Essays on Gay Life and Liberation, 1973–1977.* Boston: Union Park Press.

Gerhards, Jürgen, and Dieter Rucht. 1992. "Mesomobilization: Organizing and Framing in Two Protest Campaigns in West Germany." *American Journal of Sociology* 98:555–95.

Ginsburg, Faye D. 1989. *Contested Lives: The Abortion Debate in an American Community.* Berkeley: University of California Press.

Gitlin, Todd. 1980. *The Whole World Is Watching: Mass Media in the Making and the Unmaking of the New Left.* Berkeley: University of California Press.

Gluck, Sherna Berger. 1987. *Rosie the Riveter Revisited: Women, the War, and Social Change.* New York: Meridian.

Goldstein, Richard. 1991. "Vox Populi: When Should Media Be Involved in Outing?" *The Advocate,* August 27, 98.

Goodwin, Jeff, James M. Jasper, and Francesca Polletta. 2001. "Introduction: Why Emotions Matter." In *Passionate Politics: Emotions and Social Movements,* eds. Jeff Goodwin, James M. Jasper, and Francesca Polletta, 1–25. Chicago: University of Chicago Press.

Gould, Deborah B. 2002. "Life during Wartime: Emotions and the Development of ACT UP." *Mobilization* 7, no. 2:177–200.

Greenberg, David F. 1988. *The Construction of Homosexuality.* Chicago: University of Chicago Press.

Gross, Larry. 1993. *Contested Closets: The Politics and Ethics of Outing.* Minneapolis: University of Minnesota Press.

Gusfield, Joseph R. 1981. *The Culture of Public Problems: Drinking-Driving and the Symbolic Order*. Chicago: University of Chicago Press.

Hadden, Jeffrey K., and Anson Shupe. 1988. *Televangelism: Power and Politics on God's Frontier*. New York: Henry Holt.

Haldeman, Douglas C. 1994. "The Practice and Ethics of Sexual Orientation Conversion Therapy." *Journal of Consulting and Clinical Psychology* 62, no. 2: 221–27.

Halliday, Terence C., Michael J. Powell, and Mark W. Granfors. 1993. "After Minimalism: Transformation of State Bar Associations from Market Dependence to State Reliance, 1918 to 1950." *American Sociological Review* 58:515–35.

Harrell, David Edwin, Jr. 1988. *Pat Robertson: A Personal, Political and Religious Portrait*. San Francisco: Harper and Row.

Hendriks, Aart, Rob Tielman, and Evert van der Veen. 1993. *The Third Pink Book: A Global View of Lesbian and Gay Liberation and Oppression*. Buffalo, N.Y.: Prometheus Books.

Herman, Didi. 1994. "The Christian Right and the Politics of Morality in Canada." *Parliamentary Affairs* 47, no. 2:268–79.

———— 1997. *The Antigay Agenda: Orthodox Vision and the Christian Right*. Chicago: University of Chicago Press.

Himmelstein, Jerome L. 1983. "The New Right." In *The New Christian Right*, edited by Robert C. Leibman and Robert Wuthnow, 15–30. New York: Aldine.

Honan, William H. 1992. "Judge Overrules Decency Statute for Arts Grant." *New York Times,* June 10.

IGA (International Association of Lesbian/Gay Women and Gay Men). 1985. *IGA Pink Book*. Amsterdam: COC-magazijn.

ILGA (International Lesbian and Gay Association). 1988. *The Second ILGA Pink Book*. Utrecht: Interfacultaire Werkgroep Homostudies, Rijksuniversiteit Utrecht.

Inglehart, Ronald, et al. 2001. *World Values Surveys and European Values Surveys, 1981– 1984, 1990–1993, 1995–1997 and 1999–2000* [Computer file]. Ann Arbor, Mich.: Inter-university Consortium for Political and Social Research [distributor]. http://webapp.icpsr.umich.edu/cocoon/ICPSR-STUDY/02790.xml.

Irvine, Janice M. 2002. *Talk about Sex: The Battles over Sex Education in the United States*. Berkeley: University of California Press.

Jasper, James M. 1998. *The Art of Moral Protest: Culture, Biography, and Creativity in Social Movements*. Chicago: University of Chicago Press.

Jay, Karla. 1999. *Tales of a Lavender Menace: A Memoir of Liberation*. New York: Basic Books.

Jelen, Ted G., and Clyde Wilcox. 2003. "Causes and Consequences of Public Attitudes toward Abortion: A Review and Research Agenda." *Political Research Quarterly* 56:489–500.

Johnson, David K. 2004. *The Lavender Scare: The Cold War Persecution of Gays and Lesbians in the Federal Government.* Chicago: University of Chicago Press.

Katz, Jonathan Ned. 1995. *The Invention of Heterosexuality.* New York: Plume Books.

Kennedy, Elizabeth Lapovsky, and Madeline D. Davis. 1993. *Boots of Leather, Slippers of Gold: The History of a Lesbian Community.* New York: Routledge.

King, Brayden G., and Sarah A. Soule. 2007. "Social Movements as Extra-institutional Entrepreneurs: The Effect of Protests on Stock Price Returns." *Administrative Science Quarterly* 52:413–42.

Kirby, David. 2000. "After the Fall." *The Advocate,* November 21, 41–44.

Klatch, Rebecca E. 1987. *Women of the New Right.* Philadelphia: Temple University Press.

Kramer, Larry. 1983. "1,112 and Counting." *New York Native* no. 59 (March 14–27). Reprinted in Kramer 1994, 33–50.

———. 1994. *Reports from the Holocaust: The Story of an AIDS Activist.* New York: St. Martin's.

LaHaye, Tim. 1978. *What Everyone Should Know about Homosexuality.* Wheaton, Ill.: Tyndale House.

LaHaye, Tim F., and Jerry B. Jenkins. 1996. *Left Behind: A Novel of the Earth's Last Days.* Wheaton, Ill.: Tyndale House.

Lawton, Kim A. 1988. "Unification Church Ties Haunt New Coalition." *Christianity Today.* February 5, 46.

Levine, Martin P. 1979. "Gay Ghetto." *Journal of Homosexuality* 4:363–77.

Lewis, Gregory B., and Jonathan L. Edelson. 2000. "DOMA and ENDA: Congress Votes on Gay Rights." In *The Politics of Gay Rights,* edited by Craig A. Rimmerman, Kenneth D. Wald, and Clyde Wilcox, 193–216. Chicago: University of Chicago Press.

Lienesch, Michael. 1993. *Redeeming America: Piety and Politics in the New Christian Right.* Chapel Hill: University of North Carolina Press.

Lindsay, D. Michael. 2008. "Evangelicals in the Power Elite: Elite Cohesion Advancing a Movement." *American Sociological Review* 73:60–82.

Lippitt, Gordon L., and Warren H. Schmidt. 1967. "Crises in a Developing Organization." *Harvard Business Review* 45:102–12.

Lively, Scott, and Kevin Abrams. 1995. *The Pink Swastika: Homosexuals and the Nazi Party.* Keizer, Ore.: Founders.

Lo, Clarence Y. H. 1982. "Countermovements and Conservative Movements in the Contemporary U.S." *Annual Review of Sociology* 8:107–34.

Loftus, Jeni. 2001. "America's Liberalization in Attitudes toward Homosexuality, 1973 to 1998." *American Sociological Review* 66:762–82.

Luker, Kristen. 1989. *Abortion and the Politics of Motherhood.* Berkeley: University of California Press.

————. 2007. *When Sex Goes to School: Warring Views on Sex and Sex Education since the Sixties.* New York: W. W. Norton.

Macks, Judy, and Caitlin Ryan. 1988. "Lesbians Working in AIDS: An Overview of Our History and Experience." In *The Sourcebook on Lesbian/Gay Healthcare,* edited by Michael Shernoff and William A. Scott, 198–201. Washington, D.C.: National Lesbian/Gay Health Foundation.

Malinowsky, H. Robert, and Gerald J. Perry, eds. 1989. *The AIDS Information Sourcebook, 1989–90.* 2nd ed. Phoenix: Oryx Press.

Marcus, Eric. 1992. *Making History: The Struggle for Gay and Lesbian Equal Rights—1945–1990—An Oral History.* New York: Perennial.

Marotta, Toby. 1981. *The Politics of Homosexuality.* Boston: Houghton Mifflin.

Marsden, George. 1980. *Fundamentalism and American Culture: The Shaping of Twentieth-Century Evangelicalism 1870–1925.* New York: Oxford University Press.

————. 1991. *Understanding Fundamentalism and Evangelicalism.* Grand Rapids, Mich.: William B. Eerdmans.

Martin, William C. 1991. *A Prophet with Honor: The Billy Graham Story.* New York: William Morrow.

————. 1996. *With God on Our Side: The Rise of the Religious Right in America.* New York: Broadway Books.

McAdam, Doug. 1982. *Political Process and the Development of Black Insurgency, 1930–1970.* Chicago: University of Chicago Press.

McCarthy, John D., David W. Britt, and Mark Wolfson. 1991. "The Institutional Channeling of Social Movements by the State in the United States." *Research in Social Movements, Conflicts, and Change* 13:45–76.

McCarthy, John D., and Mayer N. Zald. 1977. "Resource Mobilization and Social Movements: A Partial Theory," *American Journal of Sociology* 82:1212–41.

McCorkle, Suzanne, and Marshall G. Most. 1997. "The Idaho Anti-Gay Initiative: A Chronology of Events." In *Anti-Gay Rights: Assessing Voter Initiatives,* edited by Stephanie L. Witt and Suzanne McCorkle, 51–62. Westport, Conn.: Praeger.

McLaren, Angus, and Arlene Tigar McLaren. 1986. *The Bedroom and the State: The Changing Practices and Politics of Contraception and Abortion in Canada, 1880–1980.* Toronto: McClelland and Stewart.

Meyer, David S., and Suzanne Staggenborg. 1996. "Movements, Countermovements and the Structure of Political Opportunity," *American Journal of Sociology* 101:1628–60.

————. 1998. "Countermovement Dynamics in Federal Systems: A Comparison of Abortion Politics in Canada and the United States." *Research in Political Sociology* 8:209–40.

Moen, Matthew C. 1995. "From Revolution to Evolution: The Changing Nature of the Christian Right." In *The Rapture of Politics: The Christian Right as the United States Approaches the Year 2000,* edited by Steve Bruce, Peter Kivisto, and William H. Swatos Jr., 123–35. New Brunswick, N.J.: Transaction Publishers.

Mohr, Richard D. 1992. *Gay Ideas: Outing and Other Controversies.* Boston: Beacon Press.

Moon, Dawne. 2004. *God, Sex, and Politics: Homosexuality and Everyday Theologies.* Chicago: University of Chicago Press.

Newman, Lesléa. 1989. *Heather Has Two Mommies.* Boston: Alyson Wonderland.

NGLTF (National Gay and Lesbian Task Force). 2007a. "Task Force History." National Gay and Lesbian Task Force. http://www.thetaskforce.org/about_us/history.

———. 2007b. "Relationship Recognition Map for Same-Sex Couples in the United States." http://thetaskforce.org/reports_and_research/relationship_recognition.

NGTF (National Gay Task Force). 1975. "Media Protest: 'Born Innocent.'" *Newsletter.* Lesbian Herstory Archives, Brooklyn. Org. Drawer 7: NGLTF.

———. 1977a. "We Are Your Children." Press release. June 13. Human Sexuality Collection, Cornell University, Ithaca, N.Y. Collection #7301, box 11.

———. 1977b. "Gay Media Alert Action Report." Press release. Human Sexuality Collection, Cornell University, Ithaca, N.Y. Collection #7301, box 11.

———. 1977c. *What to Do about Anita Bryant.* Action report. April/May. Lesbian Herstory Archives, Brooklyn. Org. File: NGLTF.

———. 1977d. Member letter. May. Lesbian Herstory Archives, Brooklyn. Org. File: NGLTF.

Norton, Rictor. 1992. *Mother Clap's Molly House: The Gay Subculture in England, 1700–1830.* London: GMP Publishers.

Oldfield, Duane M. 1996. *The Right and the Righteous: The Christian Right Confronts the Republican Party.* Lanham, Md.: Rowman and Littlefield.

Oliver, Pamela E., and Hank Johnston. 2000. "What a Good Idea!: Ideologies and Frames in Social Movement Research." *Mobilization* 5:37–54.

Ostling, Richard N. 1984. "Evangelical Publishing and Broadcasting." In *Evangelicalism and Modern America,* edited by George Marsden, 46–55. Grand Rapids, Mich.: William B. Eerdmans.

Panem, Sandra. 1988. *The AIDS Bureaucracy: Why Society Failed to Meet the AIDS Crisis and How We Might Improve Our Response.* Cambridge, Mass.: Harvard University Press.

Patton, Cindy. 1990. *Inventing AIDS.* New York: Routledge.

———. 1993. "Tremble, Heteroswine!" In *Fear of a Queer Planet,* edited by Michael Warner, 143–77. Minneapolis: University of Minnesota Press.

Pelham, Ann. 1981. "Family Protection Act: Dear to the New Right, But Unlikely to Get Out of Committee." *Congressional Quarterly Weekly,* October 3, 1916.

Penning, James M. 1995. "Pat Robertson and the GOP: 1988 and Beyond." In *The Rapture of Politics: The Christian Right as the United States Approaches the Year 2000,* edited by Steve Bruce, Peter Kivisto, and William H. Swatos Jr., 105–22. New Brunswick, N.J.: Transaction Publishers.

Perrow, Charles, and Mauro F. Guillén. 1990. *The AIDS Disaster: The Failure of Organizations in New York and the Nation.* New Haven: Yale University Press.

Persell, Caroline, Adam Green, and Liena Gurevich. 2001. "Civil Society, Economic Distress, and Social Tolerance." *Sociological Forum* 16:203–30.

PFAW (People for the American Way). 2006a. "Right Wing Organizations—Concerned Women for America." http://www.pfaw.org/pfaw/general/default.aspx?oid=22376.

———. 2006b. "Right Wing Organizations—Traditional Values Coalition." http://www.pfaw.org/pfaw/general/default.aspx?oid=8992.

Pinello, Daniel R. 2003. *Gay Rights and American Law.* Cambridge: Cambridge University Press.

———. 2006. *America's Struggle for Same-Sex Marriage.* Cambridge: Cambridge University Press.

Plant, Richard. 1986. *The Pink Triangle: The Nazi War against Homosexuals.* New York: Henry Holt.

Preslar, J. Allan. 2006. "Focusing on the Family: Three Reactions." *MinistryWatch .com.* http://www.ministrywatch.com/mw2.1/F_SumRpt.asp?EIN=953188150.

Quillan, Lincoln. 1996. "Group Threat and Regional Change in Attitudes toward African-Americans." *American Journal of Sociology* 102:816–60.

Rimmerman, Craig A. 2000a. "Beyond Political Mainstreaming: Reflections on Lesbian and Gay Organizations and the Grassroots." In *The Politics of Gay Rights,* edited by Craig A. Rimmerman, Kenneth D. Wald, and Clyde Wicox, 54–78. Chicago: University of Chicago Press.

———. 2000b. "A 'Friend' in the White House? Reflections on the Clinton Presidency." In *Creating Change: Sexuality, Public Policy, and Civil Rights,* edited by John D'Emilio, William B. Turner, and Urvashi Vaid, 43–56. New York: St. Martin's.

Robertson, Pat. 1992. "1992 Republican Convention." Address given to Republican National Convention in Houston, Texas, August 19. http://www.patrobertson.com/Speeches/1992GOPConvention.asp.

Robinson, Christine M., and Sue E. Spivey. 2007. "The Politics of Masculinity and the Ex-Gay Movement." *Gender and Society* 21:650–75.

Rochon, Thomas R. 1998. *Culture Moves: Ideas, Activism, and Changing Values.* Princeton: Princeton University Press.

Rohlinger, Deana A. 2002. "Framing the Abortion Debate: Organizational Resources, Media Strategies, and Movement-Countermovement Dynamics." *Sociological Quarterly* 43:479–507.

Rohter, Larry. 1992. "Candidate's Wife; Unrepentant, Marilyn Quayle Fights for Family and Values." *New York Times,* October 28.

Russo, Vito. 1987. *The Celluloid Closet: Homosexuality in the Movies.* New York: Harper.

Schleder, Terry. 1994. "Discrimination Costs: The Boycott Strategy." *Queer Resources Directory.* http://www.qrd.org/qrd/www/FTR/boycott.html.

Scott, Eugenie C. 1997. "Antievolution and Creationism in the United States." *Annual Review of Anthropology* 26:263–89.

Seidman, Steven. 1993. "Identity and Politics in a 'Postmodern' Gay Culture: Some Historical and Conceptual Notes." In *Fear of a Queer Planet: Queer Politics and Social Theory,* edited by Michael Warner, 105–42. Minneapolis: University of Minnesota Press.

Shepard, Benjamin Heim. 1997. *White Nights and Ascending Shadows.* London: Cassell.

Shilts, Randy. 1987. *And the Band Played On: Politics, People and the AIDS Epidemic.* New York: St. Martin's.

Signorile, Michelangelo. 1991. "The Outing of Assistant Secretary of Defense Pete Williams." *The Advocate,* August 27, 34–44.

Skocpol, Theda. 2003. *Diminished Democracy: From Membership to Management in American Civic Life.* Norman: University of Oklahoma Press.

Smith, Christian. 2002. *Christian America? What Evangelicals Really Want.* Berkeley: University of California Press.

Smith, Christian, with Michael Emerson, Sally Gallagher, Paul Kennedy, and David Sikkink. 1998. *American Evangelicalism: Embattled and Thriving.* Chicago: University of Chicago Press.

Smith, Miriam. Forthcoming. *Political Institutions and Lesbian and Gay Rights in the United States and Canada.* New York: Routledge.

Smith-Rosenberg, Caroll. 1989. "Discourses of Sexuality and Subjectivity: The New Woman, 1870–1936." In *Hidden from History: Reclaiming the Gay and Lesbian Past,* edited by Martin Duberman, Martha Vicinus, and George Chauncey, 264–80. New York: Plume Books.

Snow, David A., and Robert D. Benford. 1988. "Ideology, Frame Resonance and Participant Mobilization." *International Social Movement Research* 1:197–217.

———. 1992. "Master Frames and Cycles of Protest." In *Frontiers in Social Movement Theory,* edited by Aldon D. Morris and Carol McClurg Mueller, 133–55. New Haven, Conn.: Yale University Press.

Snow, David A., E. Burke Rochford Jr., Steven K. Worden, and Robert D. Benford. 1986. "Frame Alignment Processes, Micromobilization, and Movement Participation." *American Sociological Review* 51:464–81.

Stein, Arlene. 2001. *The Stranger Next Door: The Story of a Small Community's Battle over Sex, Faith, and Civil Rights.* Boston: Beacon Press.

Swift, Michael (pseudonym). 1987. "Gay Revolutionary." *Gay Community News,* February 15–21, p. 5.

Tarrow, Sidney. 1993. "Cycles of Collective Action: Between Moments of Madness and the Repertoire of Contention." *Social Science History* 17, no. 2:281–307.

———. 1994. *Power in Movement: Social Movements, Collective Action, and Politics.* Cambridge: Cambridge University Press.

Teal, Donn. 1971. *The Gay Militants.* New York: Stein and Day.

Thorstad, David. 1977. Untitled. Flyer. Lesbian Herstory Archives, Brooklyn. Org. File: GAA.

Tilly, Charles. 1978. *From Mobilization to Revolution.* Reading, Mass.: Addison-Wesley.

Timmons, Stuart. 1990. *The Trouble with Harry Hay: Founder of the Modern Gay Movement.* Los Angeles: Alyson Publications.

Tobin, Kay, and Randy Wicker. 1972. *The Gay Crusaders.* New York: Paperback Library.

Treas, Judith. 2002. "How Cohorts, Education, and Ideology Shaped a New Sexual Revolution on American Attitudes toward Nonmarital Sex, 1972–1998." *Sociological Perspectives* 45:267–83.

Trumbach, Randolph. 1977. "London's Sodomites: Homosexual Behavior and Western Culture in the Eighteenth Century." *Journal of Social History* 11:1–33.

———. 1989. "The Birth of the Queen: Sodomy and the Emergence of Gender Equality in Modern Culture, 1660–1750." In *Hidden from History: Reclaiming the Gay and Lesbian Past,* edited by Martin Duberman, Martha Vicinus, and George Chauncey, 129–40. New York: Plume Books.

Vaid, Urvashi. 1995. *Virtual Equality: The Mainstreaming of Gay and Lesbian Liberation.* New York: Anchor Books.

Walsh, Edward J. 1981. "Resource Mobilization and Citizen Protest in Communities around Three Mile Island." *Social Problems* 29:1–21.

Walter, Dave. 1986. "HRCF Absorbs Financially Crippled GRNL." *The Advocate,* January 7, p. 13.

Walters, Suzanna Danuta. 2001. *All the Rage: The Story of Gay Visibility in America.* Chicago: University of Chicago Press.

Weiss, Andrea, and Greta Schiller. 1988. *Before Stonewall: The Making of a Gay and Lesbian Community.* Tallahassee, Fla.: Naiad.

Werum, Regina, and Bill Winders. 2001. "Who's 'In' and Who's 'Out': State Fragmentation and the Struggle over Gay Rights, 1974–1999." *Social Problems* 48:386–410.

Wilcox, Clyde. 1992. *God's Warriors: The Christian Right in Twentieth-Century America.* Baltimore: Johns Hopkins University Press.

———. 1995. "Premillennialists at the Millennium: Some Reflections on the Christian Right in the Twenty-first Century." In *The Rapture of Politics: The Christian*

Right as the United States Approaches the Year 2000, edited by Steve Bruce, Peter Kivisto, and William H. Swatos Jr., 21–39. New Brunswick, N.J.: Transaction Publishers.

Witt, Stephanie L., and Suzanne McCorkle. 1997. *Anti-gay Rights: Assessing Voter Initiatives.* Westport, Conn.: Praeger.

Yang, Alan S. 1997. "The Polls—Trends: Attitudes toward Homosexuality." *Public Opinion Quarterly* 61:477–507.

Zald, Mayer N. 1996. "Culture, Ideology, and Strategic Framing." In *Comparative Perspectives on Social Movements: Political Opportunities, Mobilizing Structures, and Cultural Framing,* edited by Doug McAdam, John McCarthy, and Mayer Zald, 261–74. New York: Cambridge University Press.

Zald, Mayer N., and Roberta Ash. 1966. "Social Movement Organizations: Growth, Decay and Change." *Social Forces* 3:327–41.

Zald, Mayer N., and Bert Useem. 1987. "Movement and Countermovement Interaction: Mobilization, Tactics, and State Involvement." In *Social Movements in an Organizational Society,* edited by Mayer N. Zald and John D. McCarthy, 247–71. New Brunswick, N.J.: Transaction Publishers.

Index

TINA FETNER is assistant professor of sociology at McMaster University in Hamilton, Ontario, Canada.